The Extinction of Responsibility and Character

The Extinction of Responsibility and Character

Brett J. Novick

BLOOMSBURY ACADEMIC
NEW YORK • LONDON • OXFORD • NEW DELHI • SYDNEY

BLOOMSBURY ACADEMIC
Bloomsbury Publishing Inc, 1359 Broadway, New York, NY 10018, USA
Bloomsbury Publishing Plc, 50 Bedford Square, London, WC1B 3DP, UK
Bloomsbury Publishing Ireland, 29 Earlsfort Terrace, Dublin 2, D02 AY28, Ireland

BLOOMSBURY, BLOOMSBURY ACADEMIC and the Diana logo are trademarks of Bloomsbury Publishing Plc

First published in the United States of America 2026

Copyright © Bloomsbury Publishing Inc, 2026

Cover credit: © iStock/SbytovaMN

All rights reserved. No part of this publication may be: i) reproduced or transmitted in any form, electronic or mechanical, including photocopying, recording or by means of any information storage or retrieval system without prior permission in writing from the publishers; or ii) used or reproduced in any way for the training, development or operation of artificial intelligence (AI) technologies, including generative AI technologies. The rights holders expressly reserve this publication from the text and data mining exception as per Article 4(3) of the Digital Single Market Directive (EU) 2019/790.

Bloomsbury Publishing Inc does not have any control over, or responsibility for, any third-party websites referred to or in this book. All internet addresses given in this book were correct at the time of going to press. The author and publisher regret any inconvenience caused if addresses have changed or sites have ceased to exist, but can accept no responsibility for any such changes.

A catalog record for this book is available from the Library of Congress

ISBN: HB: 9781475875379
PBK: 9781475875386
ePDF: 9781475875393
eBook: 9798881868291

Typeset by Deanta Global Publishing Services, Chennai, India
Printed and bound in the United States of America

For product safety related questions contact productsafety@bloomsbury.com.

To find out more about our authors and books visit www.bloomsbury.com and sign up for our newsletters.

To my late father, Dr. William Novick, who taught me how to be a father. To my parents, who taught me the importance of hard work and values. My wife, Darla, teaches me daily how to be a better person, parent, and spouse. My children, Billy and Samantha, give me hope for a future generation with pride. Thank you to Ms. Jackie Rom for her input on parenting strategies in the United Kingdom and elsewhere around the globe. In addition, I thank the many students, parents, and educators I have worked with over the years who have taught me so much. Please know that it has been an honor to be allowed to play a small part in your lives. The many mentors in both education and life inspired me in every aspect. Finally, thank you, the reader, for taking precious time out of your schedule to read my book. I offer my sincere and deepest gratitude to all.

Contents

Preface viii

1 Responsibility: A History of Parenting and How We Got Here 1

2 Why Is Responsibility Becoming an Endangered Species? 11

3 Responsibility around the World 21

4 What Happens When Children Do Not Have Responsibility? 33

5 What Can We Do as Parents to Grow Children's Responsibility? 41

6 A Responsible School: Public Education in Schools 73

7 Too Easily Deterred: Resiliency, Self-Discipline, and Children 91

8 What Becomes of a Generation without the Ability for Responsibility or Accountability? 101

Conclusion 111

Notes 113
About the Author 128

Preface

Education and society are at a crossroads. Nearly 50 percent of educators see student behavioral issues as the most significant career stress in teaching. Concurrently, approximately 60 percent of teachers indicate they are burnt out. As a society, we are heading down a path in which we will not continue to provide a sustainable, quality public education for all.[1] Who is responsible for this: the children, the parents, education, or society? The political hot potato of responsibility in human nature has a way of being tossed in all directions with no real answers in sight. Answers are rarely found in the fog of blame and without an understanding that this is a complex issue that requires systemic solutions.

The structure of past society, parenting, and schools was such that rules and boundaries would buffet youth, and quickly, they would recognize the constraints of their role and where they fit in the structure of adult versus child. Hence, if the child were to go off track, as children often do when learning, society and the family unit would work together synergistically to push the younger generation back on the right path. The phrase "it takes a village" to raise children was an old African proverb and a necessary tool applied in the past to all youth.

Of course, it is easy to revert to the belief that the "good old days" were so much better. To look nostalgically in the rearview mirror and conclude it was better than the view from the front windshield ahead, and conclude the answer is to go backward. That would be to oversimplify what is going on. Something is amiss with our youngest generation. They are more angry, anxious, and less able to self-regulate than the preceding generations. They are less apt to develop self-discipline and become angered when forced into responsibilities. The current generation is encountering more symptoms than the average patient admitted to a psychiatric hospital in the 1950s.[2] We are seeing students who are unable to discipline themselves, take responsibility for their actions, and now experience mental health disorders that were previously reserved for adults.

Modern youth are barraged with more information in a week than previous generations received in a year (and that information is constantly monitored and harvested by social media).[3] Our youth live in a society of contrasts and extremes. They are subject to content that implies it is unacceptable to be an innocuous child, *and* they should not be responsible for the balance of their actions. In this world, they can be sheltered from consequences and tacitly given the same authority and voice at the table as their teachers, parents, and other authority figures. Children are in a structural purgatory in which they are both sheltered and exposed, given too much responsibility and not enough, treated as being immature on one side and exposed to adult problems on the other.

As educators and parents, we must be able to prepare the next generation. We do an incredible disservice if we cannot teach them what responsibilities they will bear in society. Lessons for youth cannot come from taking away the entirety of their pain for consequences or constantly coddling them. Additionally, it will not be taught if we do not let them practice navigating and comprehending life's complex labyrinth. We fail children when we do not teach them how to be independent and self-confident in a world that will not see them as the shining apple of their collective parent's eye. We are only children once, so as adults, we must be able to balance shielding children from the troubles of the adult world while nurturing the precious nature of experiencing the beauty of being a child in modern society.

Why is responsibility an endangered species in our schools and society? Is it laissez-faire parenting? Is it an ill-prepared public education system in which more parental duties are placed at the feet of the schools? Alternatively, is it the rise of social media corrupting our youth and creating epidemic levels of cyberbullying? The question is not a simple one to answer. Responsibility, or lack thereof, is an amalgamation of parenting, mental health, education, and societal issues that must be carefully teased apart to recognize how each contributes accordingly. That is the overarching goal in this book because responsibility is indeed everyone's responsibility.

1 Responsibility
A History of Parenting and How We Got Here

As children, many of us remember being awakened to the refrain, "When I was your age, I had to walk uphill to school both ways." The wisdom of parental experience is passed down to impart the element of responsibility provided by the schools of life, challenges, and hard knocks in countless such catchphrases. Most of us have learned our most important life lessons from exposure to such challenging experiences. We know that by repeated exposure to such experiences, we realize we must bend ourselves to the rules of society, as they do not simply conform to our wishes, desires, or incessant whining, unfortunately.

History is strewn with countless unnamed souls who thought the world should center around them. They tried and may even have succeeded initially at running the world from their myopic viewpoint. Many eventually became victims of societal influences that seek to maintain what is best for society versus the desires of the individual. Look at the many failed empires and dictators who sought desires and responsibility only for what they wanted and needed at the expense of all that suffered under them. They all have risen and then fallen in piles of ashes.

As infants, our understanding of the world centers on us because, without it, we would ultimately starve and die. Yet, each day we mature and become more independent represents an opportunity to understand that we revolve around society and not vice versa. Maturity is the ability to recognize that we are a piece of the puzzle of a global community and not the entire puzzle.

Many of the globe's most significant leaders were not born with a silver spoon in their mouths or given the luxury of deferring responsibility. Take Abraham Lincoln, for example; he was born in poverty, witnessed the death of his mother, and was raised by a stern father who saw no purpose in his son's education as it did little to serve in helping with the backbreaking work of harvesting crops. Young Lincoln was left to teach himself to read under the glow of the firelight. Though his father did not teach him the responsibility of education, he did teach him the importance of independence and responsibility to his family and the larger society he would be eventually released to.[1]

A more modern example is Warren Buffett. Warren Buffet began trading stocks when he was just eleven years of age. When questioned about the nature of his successes, he answered, "If every shot were a hole-in-one, it wouldn't make the game very interesting. You have to hit balls in the woods a few times to learn how to invest and lead others to performance standards."[2] What if Mr. Buffet decided that investing had too few holes in one? Or, he thought the game of investing was unfair, and he just packed up his investing clubs and gave up? The investing world would be a very different place than what exists today.

As society has evolved, technology has evolved, and parenting has changed. In the past, good parenting was measured by the ability to provide food, shelter, clothing, and love as the prerequisites for successful parenting. Much has changed in the last several decades. Let us look at how parenting and the roles of responsibility since the 1950s have evolved. I know it is way back, but it gives us a good idea of how we got to the way we parent and see society today.

Parenting in the 1950s

In the idyllic world of many of our parents and grandparents, Elvis was king, and teens in poodle skirts listened to Doo-Wop on the radio. Elvis "The Pelvis" Presley was censored on the Ed Sullivan Show for undulating his hips because it was inappropriate.[3] Yet, what was parenting like for the "Baby Boomer" Generation?

According to Dr. John Rosemond, a family psychologist, parenting was not tempered by being overly liberal or passive and took a more middle-of-the-road conservative stance.[4] The notion of "kids are seen and not heard" was adopted. Parents were not as concerned with the child's desires, and simply providing material items was not associated with good parenting. Children were responsible for seeking playdates and were encouraged to go outside and engage in unstructured activities. They needed to feel boredom and develop creative outlets to address that boredom. Most families routinely had nightly family dinners, and activities were centered around the family's schedule (not the other way around).

1960s Parenting

In the era of the moon landing and John F. Kennedy's famous speech, "Ask not what your country can do for you but what you can do for your country," parenting took a turn, paralleling the "peace, love, and rock-n-roll" generation. Children were given unprecedented freedom during this time as the family dynamic again shifted. Latchkey children were in charge of letting themselves in their homes, and they came and went without much supervision. It was a much more laissez-faire parenting attitude than just a decade previous.[5]

1970s Parenting

In the era of disco and staying out of the water because of fear of the great white shark, Jaws, parenting was dominated by what became known as "free-range parenting." In this form of parenting, unscheduled activities took precedence. Thus, socialization and unstructured time were practiced to develop social skills. Additionally, children were parented proactively versus reactively out of fear that they may get hurt and must be insulated from any potential consequences. Children were given more opportunities for freedom and responsibility based on proving their ability to handle their duties.[6]

1980s Parenting

It was a time of excess: Pac-Man, Rubik's Cubes, Cabbage Patch Dolls, neon, and spandex. The 1980s were known as the "Greed Decade" with the advent of young urban professional Yuppies (young urban professionals) looking to get ahead financially and live a lifestyle of the rich or famous.[7] Nevertheless, what was parenting like during this decade?

According to the University of Pennsylvania sociologist Dr. Annette Lareau, parents in this decade shifted to a "natural growth" parenting mindset. That is, children were provided abundant food, shelter, and love. In doing so, they were intentionally insulated from adult concerns and experiences and allowed to engage in a largely self-directed childhood free of adult concerns that they lacked the maturity or ability to address.[8]

1990s Parenting

The 1990s saw the beginning of the internet for the American consumer; the Cold War ended, the USSR. fell, and the advent of the McMansion and relative wealth, peace, and prosperity. According to NYU Psychologist Dr. Jonathan Haight was the genesis of the "Overprotective Parenting" generation.[9] The goal was well intended but had misdirected consequences.[10] This parenting aimed to protect children from the challenging world that society beset in front of them.

The problem is that, at its extreme, it fostered parenting that blurs the line between parenting and controlling. Well-meaning parents tried to insulate their children from feeling the sting of the word "no," losing or failing at something. These children never developed a mental immune system for rejection of any type. They became entitled and fell apart at the first sign of challenge or rejection. Despite parents' best efforts, they simply could not do for their children what they needed to learn and practice for themselves.

Early 2000s Parenting

The beginning of the 2000s did little to remedy any parental fear of the world's dangers. We saw 9/11, and terrorism became a danger that could seemingly crop up anywhere in the world. Society felt the vulnerability and fragility of life, and a great deal of the world's innocence broke with it. Technology and the internet became mainstream, as did email, the World Wide Web, and surfing for information.

Parents in the early part of the twenty-first century were now waiting longer to have children and thus were generally more established in their careers. For instance, in 1970, first-time mothers averaged 21.7 years of age. In the early part of the millennia, 26.7 was the average age.[11] According to University of Pennsylvania sociology professor Annette Lareau, this parenting style that transitioned through the late 1990s and into the millennium was called intensive or helicopter parenting.[12]

According to the author of *The Cultural Contradictions of Parenthood*, sociologist Sharon Hays, the parenting style was, "Child-centered, expert-guided, emotionally absorbing, labor intensive and financially expensive."[13] This style of parenting was also hallmarked by parents being highly involved in every aspect of their child's lives, parent(s) that were proactively anticipating the problems that a child may have and attempting to solve them accordingly. It also required having fewer children that were more involved in a host of structured activities to ensure that they reached their full social, cognitive, and physical potential.[14]

2010 to Present

A new super strain of helicopter parenting evolved from Covid-19: that of lawnmower parenting. Lawnmower parenting is defined by how parents "mow over" the responsibility and role children should developmentally assume to fully grow and mature. In this parenting style, parents manage to plow ahead, working on every minute aspect, rearranging—micromanaging, interfering, and arranging their children's lives.[15] They aim to protect them from any failure, disappointment, discomfort, and adversity.

Lawnmower parents try to take the sting and responsibility out of their children's lives. They may do things like do a child's homework for them, call teachers when a child does not get the grades that they want, attack others when their child has made a mistake, take a child out of activities that they feel they are not thriving in or if their child is not made to feel more special than others. In short, they will do anything to prevent their children from experiencing negative consequences of mistakes in their young lives.

It should be noted that parents who are "lawnmowering" are well-intentioned in giving their children the best future possible. That being said, children cannot learn resilience, discipline, or how to address an issue if they are not meant to feel the consequences of their actions. Additionally, if every time an issue occurs, it is taken care of by the parent, the child learns that they must have the parent to solve their problems and begins to feel helpless, which creates inherent anxiety issues. Often this is couched in the denial by these parents of "I am not the type of parent who says not my child; but it is not my child."

Another style of parenting that has come into existence is eggshell parenting. Parents are the pilots who navigate the family and set the tempo for the emotional barometer of their children. When parents do not, or cannot, maintain a stable mood, this results in unpredictability within the family. Hence, children are "walking on eggshells" to avoid their parents reacting emotionally.[16] Often, these parents are emotionally reactive to stress and cannot regulate their feelings. As a result, their anger, stress, and anxiety explode uncontrolled upon their children. In this case, children falsely believe they are responsible for their parent's emotional state. Despite being unable to change the adult's emotional state, they feel they have failed to help the parents and failed in their role as a child.

What Will the Future Parenting Style Hold?

What will the future parenting style be as we enter 2026 and beyond? That is probably anyone's guess and is likely a subject open for intense debate among sociologists, psychologists, marriage and family therapists, educators, and parents. If you look at the past few years, they have not boded well. Will our society ever feel comfortable with loosening the grip on our parenting styles and educational systems and placing responsibility back in the hands of the parents and adults?

When one thinks that we have been through a recent pandemic that occurs approximately every century, and our next generation of our next generation of prospective parents were raised after 9/11 it does not look promising. In the throes of a war on terrorism and a time when social media has many comparing who is parenting and doing other things "better" than another, it is not likely that our parenting style will become any less restrictive. That is unless consideration of the consequences of our parenting style in the ability for children to fully grow and achieve in their responsibilities is considered.

Is There Hope for a More Balanced Parenting Style?

According to clinical psychologist Dr. Shefali Tsabary, PhD, and author of *The Conscious Parent: Transforming Ourselves, Empowering Our Children*, Conscious

Parenting will be the next natural evolution of parenting.[17] In the Conscious Parenting mindset, a parent attempts to utilize an inherent awareness of the child's needs by actively listening to them and trying to find a cause and origin of how they may be acting and what the child may need to better respond to the scenarios around them. To develop increased communication and understanding, the parent acts more as a peer to the child and sets firm expectations and means of teaching self-regulation versus punishment or disciplinary sanctions.[18] The term self-regulation is a broad definition for children and adults alike that involves monitoring, evaluating, and controlling one's behavior toward a larger goal or purpose.[19]

Modern Gentle Parenting

Gentle parenting is a modern form of parenting that closely parallels permissive parenting. The fundamental principle of this style is trying to determine with our children what is causing their behavior. Additionally, gentle parenting accepts all emotions with great support and no judgment. Mutual respect and open, direct communication are critical in this paradigm.

Although this sounds great in theory, research shows that it is not the optimal approach for every child. Limits and discipline must be based on and tailored to the child's level of opposition, compliance, or defiance and the situation.

So, Which Is Best to Help a Child Develop Responsibility?

The answer to helping a child fully develop responsibility is difficult, as there is likely not one perfect answer. Parenting is not a "one size fits all" solution or a blanket statement that can be applied to various children, cultures, and situations. That being said, however, specific strategies allow for more responsibility for a child and, still others, less.

We have seen the devastating consequences of adults who perpetually never see anything as their fault and never see a problem with a solution within their grasp. They live in a world in which they are always the victim and never the victor in their life circumstances. As a result, they stall and fail when tasks or responsibilities of life are placed upon their shoulders.

The concept of responsibility will be explored further in this book. How do we teach our children at home, school, and society that they can recognize what is in their locus of control to accept, embrace, and change? What is it that we need to equip our children with so that the knee-jerk reaction of "it wasn't me" or "it wasn't my fault" does not roll off their tongues so quickly, and they can recognize problems as opportunistic blocks from which to build and climb upon.

Is Parenting Better Now than in the Past?

Parents believe today that parenting is much more complicated than ever, with 66 percent of parents noting it is more complex than it was only two decades ago. Interestingly, in modern society, parents see possible mental health issues of anxiety and depression as the number one concern that parents have in a large scale 2022 Pew Research Study of parenting.[20] Interestingly, corresponding to this parental concern is that children in the early part of the millennium youth, ages 6–17, had a formal anxiety diagnosis of 6.4 percent in 2007.[21] By 2020, 9.2 percent of children had a diagnosis of anxiety, and that trend seems to be escalating.[22] Therefore, the primary worry of children having anxiety, at least, is either a self-fulfilling prophecy, parents are more aware of what to look for, or it is a very valid concern in the realm of parenting in modern society.

Parenting may not necessarily be better or worse than it was, say, two decades or so ago. However, it is no doubt different. Parents now feel more of a need to be constantly emotionally engaged with their children and to be "hands-on" parents more than ever before. Parenting has gone from adult-centered to child-centered, which is now the dominant parenting style.[23] Hence, a parenting practice in which children's needs and wants are the central tenet of a family has become much more the norm.[24]

This, coupled with the proverbial "trying to keep up with the Joneses" due to social media, has made for a challenging and judgmental scenario in the lives of parents today. Parents now have to contend with what I call "Facebook Fables." That is, constantly comparing themselves with the imagined and perfected images of others on the internet. Thus, they are parenting their children via social media's skewed and inaccurate eye. Most people tend not to post when their child had a tantrum at Walmart, when they had a heated argument with their spouse, or when bologna and cheese sandwiches were given as dinner du jour because of a lack of time.

Instead, parents post the amazing trips, gourmet dinners that they have made, and the seemingly endless happy and joyous times of parenting (whether they are staged or not) on social media. In turn, others try to outdo each other in a technological showing of peer pressure. The isolating belief becomes that it is your family that is the only one who struggles with issues of defiance, sibling rivalry, or imperfect parenting.

The problem becomes that tantrums, parenting issues, and the challenges that influence all of us as parents are never acknowledged honestly by many out of embarrassment that they are the only ones who experiences these issues. Thus, the faulty belief becomes that no one else has common parental issues in their perfect homes.

Helpless and Hopeless—A Rudderless Child Parenting without Responsibility

As a culture, the idea of a child "being seen and not heard" certainly provides a context for the lack of a need for responsibility to be given to a child. After all, aren't they "just children" who must first grow to earn their rightful place at the table of societal and family decisions? On the flip side, in some families, children are offered decisions they are simply developmentally ill-prepared to make because they do not have the judgment or wisdom to do so.

A child not being able to begin to understand or grasp some modicum of responsibility, however, becomes helpless. Think about it: if you could not make any decisions on your own or did not have enough knowledge to be minimally competent, then what happens? What happens is that you become helpless and anxiety-ridden about every challenge that is around the corner. If you feel you cannot handle the issues in front of you, then you become hopeless and depressed. Before the Covid pandemic, both anxiety and depression were found to be increasing. By 2020, 5.6 million children (or 9.2 percent of the population) had been diagnosed with a formal anxiety disorder, and 2.4 million (or 4.0 percent of the population) had been diagnosed with a formal depressive disorder.[25] This is, of course, not inclusive of the vast numbers of youth who likely have never been formally diagnosed because they have not seen a mental health professional for treatment or diagnosis.

Mental Health on the Decline

As a final thought about parenting and responsibility, perhaps the best way to know if we have succeeded as parents is to see the status of young adults entering society. If we use this as the yardstick, we may need to readjust our parenting strategies. Looking at the generation known as Generation Z (those born between 1997 and 2012) versus the Baby Boomers (those born between 1946 and 1964), a 2024 Gallup poll indicates that only one in five of those in Generation Z report their mental health as "excellent" versus the Baby Boomers, who note 39 percent in the same category.[26]

Parents self-report that, in our present generation, more than 50 percent of adults report that the children of today's society have less quality time, are more stressed, and have worsened mental health than in any of the past generations.[27] Concurrently, one out of every six children has a diagnosable mental health issue in the United States currently, and suicide is the second-leading cause of death of children in the United States ranging from ages 10–14.[28]

2 Why Is Responsibility Becoming an Endangered Species?

Responsibility Is Bad

Responsibility has come to have a negative connotation. Think about the term "Take responsibility for your actions." What does it mean to you? It is my guess you have come to believe that "taking responsibility" means taking the helm solely for negative behavior. Most of us do not equate responsibility taking with being responsible for a new job, achieving a good grade, or doing well on a task. For that matter, neither do children, who see responsibility from a primarily negative perspective.

Common Sense and Responsibility

Our litigious society has done its best to eliminate responsibility in the fear of legal action. Take, for instance, the lawsuit of Liebeck versus McDonald's (aka the McDonald's coffee case). This case involved the reason for all coffee cups to have inscribed about caution due to hot coffee being hot.

Mistakes Are Bad, and So Responsibility Is Bad

All of us have some form of distorted thoughts. These are thoughts we process from others' communication in some faulty way. These thought processes can be based on our upbringing, personality, self-esteem, or a combination of these factors. Many of us, adults and children included, tend to harbor two tacit internal biases regarding responsibility. These cognitive mistakes are the fundamental attribution and the lesser-known actor-observer bias.

The fundamental attribution bias is how we look at what another does based on our belief in their internal characteristics, such as personality and behavior. In short, anything that happens *to us* is intentional and the result of another person trying to slight, hurt, or attack us. For instance, a child walks past another child in the school hallway, and they say hello but do not receive any response from their peer. The fundamental attribution error immediately would indicate that *the other* child was being rude, arrogant, a jerk, and so on. It would not account for the many possibilities of other external factors such as the hallways being loud, the other child not hearing them, being hard of hearing, or listening to headphones. In short, the child who simply said "hello" places the blame on the perceived internal factors of their peer's personality and inventions.

Now, let us look at it from the actor-observer bias. If the reverse were true and that other peer said hello to the child in question, and he would not have gotten a response reciprocally, then he would indicate that it was *not him* but other external factors such as the noise in the hallway, his listening to music on his headphones, distraction from looking at his phone, etcetera that kept him from saying hello to that peer in the hallway. In short, he will readily provide reasons *as external* to ourselves for our actions and see other's behavior as internal, calculating and intentional.

Thus, our bias is to blame others for the responsibility of what they do, regardless of whether some of the factors are outside their control. Alternatively, we quickly blame items outside our control rather than internal motivations where the reverse is true. The legendary comedian George Carlin perceived the idea of these twin biases ideally in a line from his stand-up routine. When driving on the highway, those who are moving faster than you are "crazy," and those who are driving slower than you are "idiots." Yet, we never think that, in another's world, we likely fall into one of those two categories as well.

A World That Allows Anonymity Fosters Lack of Responsibility

In August 1961, Yale University psychologist Dr. Stanley Milgram conducted experiments that tested the limits of human empathy and obedience. This experiment aimed to test an individual's human conscience by having forty males of varying ages and levels of education follow the orders of an established authority figure.[1] The direction was to provide ever-intensifying levels of a simulated shock to another participant in an adjacent room should they answer a question incorrectly. As each question was asked, an authority figure advised the study individuals to provide gradually increasing levels of shock to the person answering the questions. The result was as fascinating as it was frightening; the vast proportion of test subjects completely obeyed the directions, with 100 percent of the study group believing they had given a charge of 300 volts and 65 percent completing the full 450 volts (a fatal shock if implemented on an actual person).[2]

The experiment's primary objective was for Milgram to observe to what extent people would follow the commands of those presumed to be authority figures. Yet, it also displays a secondary troubling attribute: when we do not see another's pain, body language, or facial expressions, it becomes infinitely easier to exhibit behaviors we would not typically display face-to-face and thus be optimally responsible for displaying. Thus, when following orders, or having a veil of anonymity, we are more apt to shift or defer responsibility.

Looking at another more recent research experiment delved into what tends to trend most virally (i.e., most rapidly) on social media. Research by a major university in China was conducted via a Twitter-like social media site entitled *Sina Weibo*. In carefully tracking emoticons posted on the site, the researchers determined joy traveled through social media somewhat more quickly than disgust or sadness.[3] However, nothing traveled faster or more virally to users than abject rage. The high-arousal emotion of rage created proverbial wildfires in users and were further fanned by the winds of anonymity and groupthink.

What does this say for our children and society, who communicate primarily in social media and technology-based forums? Further, a study by John Suter, PhD, of Rider University, determined how a phrase coined as the Online Inhibition Effect impacts communication on the web.[4] Suter found that a synergistic combination of anonymity, lack of responsibility, and a distinct ability to disassociate one's reality from fantasy create the optimal environment for cyberbullying. A youth, or any individual, regularly disassociates when they enter the web and alter their age, create a video game profile (i.e., "an avatar"), or when people splice together their social media feeds to fabricate a life far more interesting than the humdrum grind of daily life (or what I like to refer to as "Facebook Fables").

Our next generation exists within both of the above realms with one foot in the concrete world and another in the digital realm. This anonymity allows for inflated bravery and brashness that face-to-face interactions generally do not. If you do not see another individual's reaction in real-time, you do not take the same level of responsibility for your actions, and your guilt and remorse are simultaneously lessened accordingly.[5] Less guilt comes with less responsibility for one's actions because you do not see a person I am harassing or intimidating; it is simply a name, an account, and words on a screen. Humanity is taken out of the dialogue; in fact, all aspects are seemingly dematerialized, "hosted" in "clouds" that are only in a proverbial digital ether as is one's primary responsibility to another individual's dignity and feelings.[6]

A Lack of Role Models That Want to Take Responsibility or Show Integrity

There are countless cases of those who children and society look up to who have shown a flagrant lack of responsibility and integrity in their actions. Take just one sports figure, Lance Armstrong, who was caught using illegal performance-enhancing drugs as a professional cyclist. Despite repeatedly advocating against the use of such substances, shaming those who did, and denying his own usage, he was banned after it was revealed that he used performance-enhancing drugs for the majority of his career. Further, when he was caught with performance-enhancing substances, he indicated he would have done it all over again if it meant reaching the level of fame he obtained in the professional cycling community. He was even found to have encouraged those on the US Cycling Team to follow his lead in their usage.[7]

Some sports figures do not even want to be associated as role models. Take, for instance, 76ers legend Charles Barkley. In the early 1990s, he aired a commercial for Nike that, in short, said, "I'm not paid to be a role model. I am paid to wreak havoc on the basketball court. Parents should be role models. Just because I dunk a basketball doesn't mean I should raise your kids." This was controversial at the time but a revolutionary novel way of thinking about athletes and those in the public eye in general.

If you look into politics, you can find many more examples of leaders who are of the mind to "do as I say, not as I do" mentality on both sides of the political aisle.[8] Bill Clinton's famous denial of his relationship with Monica Lewinsky and Donald Trump's denial of rebuttal of his many affairs with women are just two that come to mind. Yet, it leaves the question: if world leaders cannot be role models who are accountable and responsible, who can?

Finger Pointing Is Always Easier on the Brain

Neurologically, we are programmed to finger-point and blame rather than take responsibility. Duke University's research shows that our brains perceive negative and positive feedback differently.[9] When positive situations occur, our prefrontal cortex addresses these issues by slowly processing and mulling them over them logically. In contrast, when adverse problems arise, they are processed by the amygdala, whose job is to ring the alarm bell for fight and flight in perceived life-or-death scenarios.[10]

Hence, when we are blamed, our brains look at this as similar to an attack on our well-being and life. Because the brain sees these issues as a matter of survival, it must (and does) respond within a matter of milliseconds, leading us to reactive responses versus proactive, well-thought-out answers toward negative scenarios. Often, our reaction may initially be executed with little forethought or cognition when we react, and it may be to swiftly blame others for causing the issue at hand. As an example of this theory in action, remember how much easier it is to remember those you believe wronged you versus the many other times when people advocated and acted positively on your behalf. Which of these lists can you more readily recall?

Worse yet, like a common cold, blaming can be contagious to others in a family, workplace, or society. Four studies in the *Journal of Experimental Social Psychology* examined whether blame could transfer from one person to another.[11] It was found that when a single person witnessed another blaming another, they were much more likely to blame someone for their own behaviors. Studies in healthcare systems have found that when blame contagion dominates an organization, it leads to a significant decrease in trust and desire to work as a team.[12]

Apathy and Responsibility in the World of Customer Service

We all have had the experience of trying to contact a utility, cable, or other large company and felt the white-hot anger of being patronized or the representative on the other line being apathetic to our plight. When we call about a miscalculated bill or a service disruption, we are often met with a person on the other side with a script to respond to your complaint. Usually, the script includes something like "I am sorry that you are dealing with this," yet the inflection and tone indicate that this is what is said to all customers and lacks any sincerity or genuine empathy. This is, of course, if we are lucky enough to get a live agent and not an artificial intelligence rendering of what good customer service should represent.

We are left frustrated because we feel that no one takes responsibility for our mistakes nor seems to care for us as an individual customer. According to the United States Bureau of Labor Statistics, the average customer call center has a turnover of 30–45 percent, twice that of other company departments. Within a company apathy and lack of responsibility lead to a bad experience for consumers and employees alike. Relationships require a two-way expression of sincere empathy and responsibility, which is lacking in today's world. Loyalty and commitment are becoming ever less common and endangered. Responsibility is to do what is best at the moment and not about long-term dedication.

Fake News

As children enter later elementary and middle school, they learn about the hazards of gossip. Statements with a kernel of truth, or none, are spread throughout a school community faster than a virulent stomach virus. Children may sometimes be the host, target, or patient zero of these harmful statements. The hope is that children realize that these statements are primarily false and that gossip and rumors create pain for those who are at the end of these accusations.

Of course, social media gossip and rumors take on a completely new meaning because of how quickly and effectively they can be spread. Worse yet, those who are the targets of these attacks and are emotionally devastated are not seen directly by those who spread the rumors, and responsibility for one's actions is left in a diffuse fog of social media anonymity.

So, who is responsible for telling us truthful stories and news about the world around us? Usually, we entrust the media to understand the state of the world around us, both locally and globally. As we become ever-dependent on digital forms of new media, we find more and more sources, and we are left to question the accuracy of our news. Terms like bots (which make anonymous posts without human intervention), trolls (who intentionally post inflammatory and/or untrue news stories to evoke anger and avoid productive discussion), and bonnets (who try to inflate the popularity of a new inaccurate story make news and information less and less accurate).[13] Hence, we have a world that provides less precise news stories, popularizing news that may only be partially true, and others agitating and enraging people to bring out emotion, not logic, in our dialogue.

Our children see a world from a new paradigm that is inaccurate, increasingly partisan, and divided, and parents act out of emotions versus questioning the truth of the stories. The question never becomes who is responsible for an inaccurate or blatantly untrue story as everyone is too busy debating an issue that has little truth or substance and only serves to tap into the emotional agitation of its readers. Now, we can post information with no responsibility for the accuracy of its content and this is a strategy being adopted by the next generation as well.

Apathy and Modern Society

The disability advocate, author, and activist Helen Keller mused, "Science may have found a cure for most evils, but it has found no remedy for the worst of them all apathy of human beings." Apathy, at its very worst, can be a depressive symptom. Post-Covid-19, the number of adults with depressive symptoms grew from 193 million globally to 246 million.[14] Even at its best, however, apathy makes it difficult for empathy, or responsibility, to take hold fully.

Due to the internet, the average child is swarmed with 74 GB of information daily, growing by 5 percent yearly. In the 1500s, what we were subjected to in a single day was the equivalent amount of information an educated person would have learned in an entire lifetime.[15] The result? This information overload makes it difficult to focus on a single item, person, or situation. We cannot pay attention, empathize, or decide on any one area or thought because we are simply bombarded with too much data.

As a result, news events that are far away or do not directly impact us are not considered and are diverted from our thinking. Since it is too difficult to care about any one item, we tune out vast quantities of information (much more than we tune in to). Concurrently, 10 percent, or 6.1 million children, are diagnosed with ADHD (Attention-Deficit/Hyperactivity Disorder), and that number is rising.[16] Although many of these ADHD diagnoses are presumably accurate, they also coincide with the analogy of children trying to drink water from a proverbial firehose of information being spewed at them by the day, hour, and minute.

The Easy Way Out

Without responsibility, it becomes far more acceptable to simply take the easy way out of problems for children (as well as adults). Taking the easier way out points to a deeper issue for our children: a growing lack of self-discipline. The lack of this skill to take responsibility to regulate themselves toward working to a higher goal can lead to several ancillary issues. A child becomes quickly overwhelmed and unable to prioritize or plan in school, at home, or socially. They become fearful of failing, so they avoid any situation involving any possibility of failure. They steer clear from doing something if they do not believe they will receive immediate rewards for their actions (as many of the most significant and gratifying rewards require). Managing their time becomes challenging as well as they procrastinate or have trouble setting aside time to do quality schoolwork or complete chores.[17]

Too Much Responsibility and Not Knowing What to Do with It

In the typical family hierarchy of the past, children are below the parents and adults in terms of the chain of command. The parents ultimately make the decisions, using their wisdom to determine the direction the family unit should follow. As parents are the breadwinners, they have knowledge and responsibility for items such as mortgages, rent, utility bills, and marital and parental relationship issues and concerns. When these boundaries and hierarchies are disturbed, it creates problems for the children and the family.

In our society, children have no control over items such as mortgages, rent, utility bills, or a firm understanding of marital and parental obligations and responsibilities. Yet, when they are voluntarily allowed or forced to jump the boundaries of adulthood and provide this information, they have little opportunity to influence these matters. This creates the ideal prescription for anxiety, as they are helpless to do anything about, nor fully comprehend, this information relayed to them and simultaneously feel somehow responsible for addressing these issues.

Some of these children become what is known as parentified. When a child is parentified, they are placed in the role of the adult without recognizing it. These children may feel responsible for their parents' emotions and feelings, for their siblings' well-being, and for placing their valuable childhood aside.[18] Issues that last a lifetime in a child's relationships can ensue from being raised in this volatile parental dynamic. Often, parentified children feel responsible for caring for everyone, may feel underappreciated when others do not return their efforts in relationships, and may constantly avoid conflict in favor of sacrificing for peacemaking with others as children and well into adulthood.[19]

You Are Darned If You Do and Darned If You Don't

Sometimes, children are inadvertently thought of as simply "little adults." This cannot be further from the truth, as children communicate differently than adults, depending on their developmental level and circumstances. Young children are very concrete little beings, so they often process what we teach them and the lessons they learn very differently from what we think we are conveying.

For example, if you watch a child spill a glass of milk and ask them if they did it, the answer will likely be "no." It is not a matter of dishonesty generally but what is known as a double bind. In a double bind, whatever I do, I will not make my parents happy. If I say that I spilled the milk, I get in trouble. If I deny spilling the milk, I will be in trouble for lying. The choices are not at all options, so the child is unable or afraid to make a decision. Many children will hedge their bets and go with the lie as it has a better chance (logically) of no consequence for their actions.

Entitlement and Its Effect on Society

One issue we hear repeatedly is that the next generation seems to have a sense of entitlement. That is, they have an inflated belief that they deserve something simply because they want it. This behavioral thought process leads to increased issues of selfishness, a marked decrease in empathetic behaviors toward others, and lack of being able to work in a team-based environment.

Research indicates that those families that have more wealth tend to be at even greater risk for feelings of entitlement.[20] Entitlement, however, does not just mean you believe you are entitled to anything you want; it also means you are entitled to not follow the restrictions of society that you don't want either. Therefore, if one feels entitled they feel that they are not responsible for the rules that they don't feel apply to them. Recent studies have indicated that the recent generations of millennials score higher on psychological scales of entitlement than any of the previous generations.[21] This is exacerbated by the widening chasm between the wealthy and poor. Take for instance that in 1980, the top income household made nine times that of those at the bottom. By the year 2018 that number was 12.6 times, a 39 percent increase.[22]

3 Responsibility around the World

Education around the World

Many Americans, with a zeal for patriotism, see our country as the best in the world in every domain. While the United States is considered the most significant economic and military powerhouse globally, it is dangerous to arrogantly believe we are "the best at everything" because it stagnates our ability to learn and grow from other countries and cultures.[1]

How do we know we have the best means of raising children? Fate placed us in our culture, country, and within our family dynamic. This has inherently created potential limits in our thinking because we have learned our ways of the world based primarily on what we have seen modeled and accepted as a cultural standard. What if you were born or grew up in a different part of the world, from a different family or culture? How would your viewpoints and perspectives change?

Take, for example, public education from kindergarten to twelfth grade in the United States; the 2020 PISA rankings, which looks at fifteen-year-olds' reading, math, and science skills, indicate that the United States ranked thirty-eighth in reading, twenty-fourth in math, and thirty-first in science versus such top-performing countries as Singapore, South Korea, and China.[2] Is it that we are doing something wrong or are other countries doing something better?

Many reasons can be pointed out for this growing educational chasm in our country, such as a lack of school funding in certain states, the increased emphasis on standardized testing as well as standardized curriculum, and socioeconomic inequality among those in our next generation. That being said, what aspects are within our responsibility and control for our children as parents and teachers? Further, what can we learn from our global community so that our children inherit a world where they can compete instead of struggle? In this section, we will look at these questions from a worldwide view rather than myopically focused on our region of the world.

Exposure to Divergent Viewpoints

One way to teach responsibility to the next generation is to allow them to develop their viewpoints and understand the notion that others have divergent perspectives. Debate and conversation are how we develop critical thinking skills, learn empathy for others, and create a broad paradigm of the world around us.[3] Without this dialogue we remain in our comfort zone and never learn nor grow.

For instance, in countries such as the Netherlands, over thirty-six different types of private, public, and religious schools are funded. Regardless of the kind of school, however, they are all required to discuss the theory of evolution (among other subjects), even if the school is creationist in the background and does not inherently believe nor adopt evolutionary theories.[4] The goal of the Netherlands' educational system is not to support or disprove evolution but to educate the population on the theory with the objective of having a well-rounded view of all potential alternative perspectives. To be fully educated, one must also understand the alternative thought processes to their own that exist (including those that are contrary to one's view). That said, teachers must refrain from establishing their judgments in place of the students or diverging from the established curriculum.

Japanese Education of the Heart

Japanese workers are known to have a substantial degree of responsibility and loyalty to their places of employment—many Japanese work up to 100 hours per week and stay committed to one workplace. The Japanese workforce rarely uses their designated sick or personal days. There is a term called *Ganbaru,* which translates as pushing yourself to your limits on behalf of the responsibility of your workplace. As a direct result, there is a term called *karoshi*, in which workers literally work themselves to death.[5]

What can we learn from such a system regarding teaching our students responsibility? The Japanese community also teaches other terms, such as *wa*, which encourages its citizens to consider the group and society's needs over those of the self. Responsibility, then, is not an individualistic "every man/woman for himself" but a concern for the many that outweighs the needs of the individual. This is in contrast to our Western very individualistic society.

In Japan's public educational school setting, *koro-no-kyoiku* is roughly translated as "education of the heart." Beginning in elementary school, integrity and morality in one's society are woven into all Japanese public school curricula. Instead of focusing solely on students taking responsibility for themselves, the goal is to be a responsible citizen of one's society. From the beginning of their education, students learn the importance of equality, creating harmony and trust in relationships, and exerting effort to their society and community.

Teaching responsibility to one's society is not done in a single assembly program or as a collateral aspect of the curriculum, as it may be in some public schools in the United States. Instead, elementary schools dedicate over thirty hours of instruction to teaching responsible decision-making and developing self-discipline and compassion. The goal of responsibility is loyalty to the group and society.[6]

Further, Japanese society calls for children to be independent at a surprisingly early age. By kindergarten, students are expected to take public transportation by themselves. This would make most American parents gasp in fear and trepidation about how a young child could take on such a dangerous task. Yet, they do this in a manner that is via a gradual acclimation of responsibility and independence. The procedure involves a systematic process of parents holding the child's hand along the route for several weeks, looking for persons who are entrusted in the community that they can engage with along the way if needed for assistance, the parent standing behind the child as they walk along, and, finally, independence. Safety is highlighted along every step of their trip to and from school, with the community providing designated safe places, homes, and stores for youth to access help, numerous crossing guards, and society banding together to blend safety and independence for all children in this procedure. The "it takes a village" approach is an essential aspect in the success of childhood independence.

The culture sees the school as an embodiment of home, and the school's cleanliness and functioning are the responsibility of all its citizens. Hence, in elementary school, students are responsible for cleaning the entire school themselves, whereas, in the United States, a good deal of this may fall upon a custodian. This skill is reinforced at home, and gradually, more challenging tasks are provided as a child has the developmental and physical milestones to do so.[7] The idea being that if you make a mess you are responsible for cleaning it up.

Would such a teaching of responsibility and independence for our children work in the United States? Probably not, due to the dynamics of American society and our unfortunate inability to trust the world as safe for our children. The point, however, is that we certainly can see the independence children are capable of at a young age, and we could learn from a gradual means of teaching our children independence from this and other societies.

Japanese and Other Cultures Encourage Intergenerational Responsibility

In the United States, it is relatively rare for more than two generations to live together for extended periods (except the typical nuclear family). According to the Pew Polls, in 2021, the number in the United States was a mere 18 percent of multigenerational families.[8] Yet, in other cultures, such as the Japanese, Indian, and Chinese cultures, intergenerational bonding and residing together are relatively standard. This family dynamic creates what researchers Brubaker and Brubaker call the 4 R's.[9] Respect, Reciprocity, Responsibility, and Resilience transmitted to all members of the family system and a byproduct of these types of extended family situations.[10]

Children learn from this living arrangement that they have close intergenerational bonds and are responsible for all family members, young and old. They understand this not by mere words but by their parents' and grandparents' actions and interactions. Additionally, they know the resiliency of previous generations by hearing the family genealogy and perspectives of the older generation(s) firsthand. In our culture generations live apart from each other and do not often have the same sense of responsibility from generation to generation.

Bildung and Why the Nordic School Systems Are So Successful

When looking at public educational systems worldwide, Nordic countries repeatedly come out on top.[11] Along this vein, when surveys of the globe's happiest societies are conducted, these countries also rank at the top of these lists.[12] Therefore, what can we learn about educating our children and teaching responsibility from this region?

The educational system's moral base is centered on the German concept of *Bildung*. What is *Bildung*? It does not have a word that has an English equivalent. However, the idea is rooted in the basis that individuals should have the foundational knowledge to thrive in their society and the maturity to be independent while simultaneously be able to work as a team within the grander framework of society.[13] In this case, responsibility is both an individual and collaborative paradigm.

The curriculum is didactic or closely intertwined with the lessons of *Bildung*. The goal of didactic learning is not to teach rote concepts. Instead, the goal is to have students experience not "what" they should know but "how" they should process the information they are provided in the world around them. These become the basis for three foundational questions for responsibility in Nordic education: what should children know, what these children should be working toward in becoming fully actualized human beings and what should they be taught to be responsible for as eventual contributing citizens?[14] These questions are not separate curriculum from concepts of social-emotional learning or character education as in the United States. Instead, they are interwoven into every aspect of a student's learning.

Netherlands Happiness in Nothingness

The Netherlands consistently also ranks as one of the happiest countries in the world. The country is well above that of the United States (the United States currently ranks fourteenth) in this category. One of its philosophies is that of *niksen*, or the art of simply doing nothing. Doing nothing involves being comfortable, calm, and regaining one's well-being.

Children in the United States are perpetually bored. They do not know how to handle doing nothing. If given the time to do nothing, they fill that vacuum with primarily technology. They cannot self-regulate themselves and rely on parents to fill their free time. Parents often oblige by filling their time with activities every evening, such as sports or other events. Yet, doing nothing can be a joint activity between families, such as reading quietly together or simply conversing.

Children learn the most about themselves and how to be creative in this time of quiet introspection. This also teaches discipline and patience, as when one cannot get what they want immediately and must acclimate to not needing to be entertained every moment of every day by parents, activities, or technology.

The UK Teaches Finding the Forest for the Trees

When we gaze into the realm of nature, we see the ultimate examples of responsibility. If a baby hatchling is mature enough, it is tossed out of the nest to fly. If it cannot spread its wings, it crashes to the ground and becomes a meal for the abundance of creatures that wait on the forest floor. Mother Nature is unforgiving regarding responsibility for all creatures of the woods, big or small.

The UK recognizes that the world of nature has much to teach about the logical and natural laws within our environment. Along this vein, over 200 so-called Forest Schools have developed in the UK since the 1990s. These "schools" represent an experience that employs the outdoors as a proverbial educational classroom. The experiences, consequences, and understanding of the definition of responsibility in these domains exist outside the realm of parental or societal involvement.

Learning is child-centered, and risk-taking as well as problem-solving are all-natural byproducts that these educational programs employ. This shift is dynamic in a world where a new generation is less inclined to embrace the outdoors. Perhaps the Forest Schools and the natural world have something we can borrow to teach our youth about responsibility from what are truly *natural* consequences.

Letting Kids Be Kids: Teaching Responsibility in India

With the increase of social media, America has developed a pandemic case of a "one-upping" mentality. A recent study indicates that 66 percent of parents have found that social media has increased the pressure to be so-called "perfect parents."[15] This has created a society in which our children are often saddled with nightly activities every night after school. From karate to art classes, dance, and music, children are booked solid with activities in the United States.

For some, the goal is to develop a sport that they may become so adept at that they may be able to one day earn a scholarship, become a more balanced and disciplined individual, or bolster social skills with peers. Yet, according to Dr. Yuko Munakata at the University of Colorado, Boulder, recent studies suggest the opposite may be valid. The more time children spend in extracurricular activities, the less proficient they are in cognitive skills such as problem-solving, decision-making, and responsibility for thinking and actions.[16] Most of our children will not see the realization of that scholarship or professional sports contract.

In India, they take a completely different route, emphasizing unstructured playtime as the primary parenting strategy.[17] The question may be asked about how this establishes responsibility in a child without any notable structure? The answer may be that learning the goals of socializing, emotional expression, and conflict resolution comes *from* practicing these skills. Social and emotional learning can be garnered somewhat from structured activities; however, these are just replications of what a child does in school. Namely, a teacher teaches, and the student passively listens. The time for proper practical socialization in the school is when adults are less present, such as at lunch and recess (at the primary and elementary levels) and playdates.

Practicing what works socially in a playdate environment requires the ability to think creatively and independently simultaneously. Through free play, youth can have facets of control usually reserved only for adults. They can be responsible for testing out if their theories of the world work in reality, taking tangible risks, and experimenting with how the world looks socially. Additionally, they can fail without the fear of adult reprisal or criticism.

In the crush of standardized testing and curriculum in the public schools world, play is crushed into ever-smaller increments of time. Yet many studies indicate that children taking responsibility for their environment via play is an effective format for learning. One of the most effective educational systems in the world, Finland, provides a fifteen-minute break for every forty-five minutes of schoolwork.[18]

"Saving Face" and Responsibility in the Chinese Family Unit

In China, children are raised with their primary responsibility to their family's reputation versus their individualistic responsibilities. A child's expression of individual emotional expression of responsibility is avoided as it may interfere with the overall harmony of the family system.[19] It is considered the right and responsibility of parents of *all* Chinese children to demonstrate authority over children by society as a whole.[20] The child, conversely, is taught to respect elders' rules, and Chinese parents are verbally critical and tend not to "sugar-coat" criticism as in the Western way of parenting. In doing so, the Asian parental perspective is that the child's psyche is solid enough to be capable of handling recrimination.[21]

In Chinese culture, academic success is often an expectation wielded via strict discipline and rules. In this way, children learn to discipline themselves toward academic achievement by recognizing the need to prioritize school above other outside activities.[22] Additionally, in traditional American cultures, parents may say things such as labeling one of their children as "bright, gifted, or talented," indicating that the child has some intrinsic talent that makes them destined for success.

Chinese parents tend to point out and sharpen a child's effort versus inherent ability is what defines their successes academically and otherwise. This is also fostered by Chinese students being taught to work together as a team toward mutual objectives in typical Chinese culture. In traditional American society, academics encourage teamwork, but ultimately, the goal is for a grade to compete with the individuals within your classroom circle.

The societal concept of "saving face" is critical in Chinese culture and parenting. The Chinese hierarchy fosters that those who are older or of higher social status should be treated with respect without question, and harmony in the family is preserved most critically. Family issues should not be aired in public as they can cause a family to "lose face" within society. How does a child or family "gain face" then? Only if children have marked achievements or contribute significantly to the community at large.[23]

Vietnam and Responsibility for Potty Training

In our modern society, we tend to assume that infants cannot, and perhaps should not, be responsible for anything. Questions are often asked about when to calm a crying baby, and experts differ based on preserving the child's burgeoning fragile self-esteem. Yet, in Vietnam, babies as young as nine months are responsible for using the bathroom independently. How is this even possible?

According to a *Journal of Pediatric Urology*, forty-seven Vietnamese parents were studied and indicated from the very first day of birth, they monitor body language, facial features, and cries for patterns of when the infant may need to use the bathroom. The mother then makes a whistling sound when the infant is going to the bathroom. By nine months, the infant pairs the sound with using the bathroom. The point? Infants in Vietnam are given responsibility for a task that we in the United States struggle with, a child taking responsibility until at least two years of age or older.

Eating, Overeating, and What We Can Learn from France

Obesity is an epidemic in the United States; according to the CDC, 19.7 percent of youth are considered obese. The United States exists in a world of perpetual super-sizing of food that has steadily increased since the 1970s. As a result, fast-food vendors and suppliers have seemingly wrestled the responsibility for youth health from the hands of parents and into a mindset that seems out of the control of parents and families to handle independently.

In the United States, many parents dismiss the well intended aspiration of feeding children regular nutritional meals, but they classify their children into the stubborn category of "finicky" eaters. Others say their kids simply refuse to eat certain foods due to preferences, a fear of vegetables, an adverse reaction to various textures, etc. Yet, if one were to look for a familiar thread that weaves through most children's diets in the United States, one would find a common trend of an affinity for a selection of foods for children, such as pizza, french fries, chicken nuggets, mac and cheese, and cheeseburgers.

What are so-called "kids' meals?" Many are the chicken nuggets, cheeseburgers, and french fries—the same foods children consider preferable to their palates. Pair this with the fact that these meals are often associated with bright-colored boxes, activities, and toys, and it is no wonder why these high-fat, high-calorie, high-carbohydrate meals are considered much more preferable to American children.

Teaching Children Structure by Action in France

In French culture, boundaries are established clearly and early.[24] The boundaries that established are what is acceptable and unacceptable in social situations. French parents are much more likely to utilize an authoritarian parenting style. In the United States, we are more apt to choose a democratic parenting style. However, a careful balance of authority and understanding can lead to a solid framework for children's expectations and their ability to understand their place within the greater family structure.[25] Thus, it is clear what the responsibility of the child and the parents are. When these roles are obvious, it helps to establish a sense of safety because the child knows what is within their ability to control and what is not.

Even in infancy, French parents leave it upon the infant to have some part in the responsibility to self-soothe. For instance, when an infant cries out, the choice is to pick them up or take a wait-and-see attitude immediately. This allows the baby to learn the responsibility of self-soothing. If not, it will be the parents' job to constantly soothe the child, which can last well past infancy.

It is also noted that when parents cater to every whim of the infant, they lose vital sleep, and their marital relationship and stamina suffers. Further, their ability to balance being a parent with being a husband, wife, spouse, or partner is impacted. Thus, preserving the family balance is crucial compared to giving in to every whim of one's children. Keeping a homeostatic balance prevents any family member from usurping the needs of all other family members; no matter the age.

In the United States, we tend to control our toddlers by keeping them in strollers. It makes corralling them that much easier in public. Yet, those in France generally stop using strollers at two or three years old. For safety and convenience, those in the United States may keep children close to the hip via strollers. It is an exciting example of how parents take on the responsibility of navigating independently much earlier versus those in the United States.[26]

Teaching Children to Sink or Swim

Of course, not just cultures around the globe have something to say about child responsibility and parental and society's role. Dr. Wendy Mogel, psychologist, and author of *The Blessing of a B Minus: Using Jewish Teaching to Raise Resilient Teenagers*, indicates that the Talmud (the central text of Judaic religious doctrine) urges parents to teach their children how to swim.[27] Essentially, this is not just a religious sanction for what a child should be able to do when faced with a body of water. Instead, children should be able to face obstacles proficiently, survive, and thrive, versus drowning in what life and society may throw at them.

So, Which Culture Has the Best Parenting Style for Children to Gain Responsibility and Independence?

The point of looking at various cultures and parenting styles is not to seek the "best" parenting style but to adopt a parenting enrichment style that works best for your family and adds additional tools to the proverbial tool belt. Just like personality types, parenting styles each have strengths and drawbacks. However, many parenting styles have some or many aspects, that can be productive and impactful in helping children attain independence and responsibility. Yet, we are often unaware of these because we simply have not been exposed to the various cultural and regional paradigms each parenting style may offer.

4 What Happens When Children Do Not Have Responsibility?

Responsibility Goes Hand-in-Hand with Self-Esteem

There are several reasons why youth need to be given age-appropriate responsibilities as they mature developmentally. One key rationale is the simple concept of growing self-esteem and confidence. If children are never allowed to test and strengthen their wings and abilities, they may never recognize that they can fly. Worse yet, they may never believe in their abilities to stretch their proverbial wings and try.

If children don't ever try to do the things they may be capable of, they become hopeless. They believe what is the sense of even trying if they cannot, or have never tried, whatever challenging task they have in front of them. In short, they have already failed before the attempt.

Whether that activity may be school, sports, or making friendships, it seems frustratingly just out of their reach or abilities. They do not test this theory for accuracy, or are kept from trying from overprotective but well-meaning parents. As a result, they never attempt to build the discipline to practice, improve, and bolster skills in any challenging domain. Instead, they continue down a rabbit hole of frustration and disbelief. This hopelessness and frustration turn inward and quickly develop into lingering sadness and depression.

When these same children feel hopeless, they also begin to believe they cannot do anything to change any situation they may encounter. The child becomes seemingly helpless about controlling any element of the world around them. Anxiety and worry ramp up as youth feel unable to control anything that spins around them. This cycle, unaddressed, can lead to a diagnosable anxiety disorde as perception of lack of control is the basis for anxiety.

Children may "finger-point" at others and refuse to see their role in any problem. Alternatively, tantruming as a behavioral means to get what they want may be employed. They may act out of perceived anger or retreat in fear. Some may regress and act less maturely as they struggle to find their role in the world.

What Do Youth Have Responsibility For?

In past generations, the saying was, "Children should be seen and not heard." Yet a child not heard is a child largely unseen by society. Indeed, in the past, these silenced children were the most significant targets and victims of innumerable counts of abuse of all kinds. Take, for instance, the need in 1938 to institute child labor laws to prevent youth essentially being used for slavery. Further, child protection agencies were set up to protect youth as they are the arguably most easily exploited of all populations.

Children represent those in our society with the least control over their lives and are the most vulnerable. What can a youth control in their lives? Not really very much: what they will wear, what they will eat, if and when they will use the bathroom, if and when they will go to sleep, and how they will behave. Without responsibilities, they tend to maladaptively hold resolutely to these attributes because it is all they have.

What does this look like? A child who feels diminished responsibility and control in their world correlates with a child who demonstrates maladaptive behaviors. They hold tight to what minor aspects of life they can control to get their point(s) across in alternative ways. They may use behaviors such as finicky eating, crying, oppositional acting-out, toileting issues, or sleep disruption to adopt some responsibility in their minimal scope of control in society.

When Nothing Is Your Fault

If children perpetually see nothing as their fault, they develop another issue that goes hand in hand: an inability to solve problems independently. Why?

If nothing is a child's fault, they cannot recognize what they can do to solve a problem. Concurrently, they do not know how to facilitate a solution to issues for which they seem they were never a part of the problem to begin with.

Yet, relationships of any type are rarely a single interactive experience. Relationships are, naturally, two-way dialogues that build upon each other and are the responsibility of both parties. Young children tend to be egocentric because they see themselves as the center of the universe around which the world revolves. As they mature and enter school, they should see that relational dynamics are building blocks built by both parties. Those who cannot take responsibility cannot understand empathy because they see things from the myopic one-way street of "not my fault, not my problem, not my job to understand things from your perspective."

These point to two issues then: responsibility and empathy. When an adult asks a child about a problem, and the child is not required to see things from the perspective of another, they do not gain that necessary ability to empathize. They are left in that constant immature emotional state of being egocentric and seeing the world revolving around them. The parent who is constantly blaming the external world supports this and also fails to help them grow emotionally. Unfortunately, the child cannot control the extrinsic world outside them that they are blaming for their plight. They never, however, learn that they should be managing and focusing on the intrinsic domains of their behavior and attitude for real change and emotional growth

When You Have No Responsibility You Believe the World Serves You

Children can also become naturally self-centered if they never have to take responsibility for anything while growing up. The world revolves around what they want, so they anticipate being given anything they desire with little challenge or effort. When others do not give them this, they do not take responsibility for their behavior. They tantrums and carry on because it becomes it is an easy "go to" habit.

Additionally, empathizing is difficult if you always see things myopically from your perspective. Empathy is about going out of oneself and feeling things from another's perspective (impossible if you cannot see it from another's vantage point). A child given everything and having responsibility for nothing will also see their viewpoint as always correct; they are never wrong.

Conversely, anyone who disagrees with them is perpetually wrong because their opinion is the only one worth valuing. Because they see everyone else as always at fault, they cannot take responsibility because there is always someone else to blame, and the finger is constantly pointing at their friends, teachers, parents, etc. This also creates an ancillary issue in that they cannot take criticism for their actions nor learn from them. These children will be prone to a continued cycle of failure and frustration because they cannot, or do not, want to understand from others how, or why, to change their behaviors.

If the world serves you, the rules that apply to you are also are at your service. Those rules that do not meet your needs at the time can be discarded as mere inconveniences. Along this vein of thought, you can rationalize away any rule that does not suit you and is unnecessary to follow or address. As you grow closer to adulthood it can change to a violation of laws or a reason to not adhere to social norms.

The All-Inclusive Vacation of Childhood

Imagine, for a moment, the perfect vacation. Most of us would seek an all-inclusive vacation with all the food, beverages, and recreation we could possibly want. When we wanted to, we could rest and sleep late; if we chose to do so we would go to planned recreational activities of our choosing. We likely would wish not to be reminded of the responsibilities of work, chores, or everyday life tasks because of the stress such activities create.

Now imagine that all of a sudden, amid your all-inclusive vacation, you were told it was time to go home, and no more all-inclusive vacation for you. It might well be that you would be upset and disappointed that you have to go home. It is likely you would look with dread at the anticipation of having all the work and chores that have piled up for you to do upon your return. What motivation would you have to return to your real life? Maybe you could extend your trip infinitely and never return to your everyday life?

Let us look at a child's example of an all-inclusive vacation; you can wake up as late as you want to, play video games, watch YouTube videos for unlimited periods, and get free snacks out of the unlimited snack bar of the refrigerator. What kid would not want that? When you are tasked with going to school, doing chores, or any other responsibility, wouldn't you choose the all-inclusive vacation of your bedroom? Further, if you are suspended from school or sent to your room, that is where you want to be anyway because, remember, it is "an all-inclusive vacation." This process can continue until parents have an eighteen- to twenty-one-year-old (or beyond) who stays in their room and is unmotivated to find a job or go to college. The ultimate question is, why would they want to go out and get a job? What motivation lights the fire of possible change? Quite simply? Nothing.

The Martyr Complex: Always the Victim Never Responsible

If you are not responsible for your behaviors, you become a victim of all circumstances surrounding you. It is not your fault for anything; everyone is out to target you in this mode of thinking. Never taking responsibility for your actions means you are the punching bag for others' ill-fated intentions and always the one with the "bad luck." Children like this are always seeking negative attention or feeling sorry for themselves, and when they reach adulthood interpret themselves as the perpetual victims of others' constant ill will.

It may seem that these children are always self-sacrificing for others in the name of their own victimhood. However, in doing so, they suffer from self-esteem issues and an inability to regulate their emotions independently of peers or authority figures' emotions. They always give others their proverbial lunch and starve themselves for their own needs in the name of being good.[1]

Parents can support their emotional growth by helping these children become more assertive in their actions and avoiding allowing their feelings of self-pity to cloud their self-esteem. Children must adaptively balance in the gray area between aggression and passivity; namely through assertion. This middle ground is what is necessary for development of appropriate conflict resolution skills.

We Are All Too Critical of Criticism

The world of our children has become such that criticism is a bad thing. Productive criticism and feedback allow a child to learn, adapt, and change direction. Children must be able to know that criticism, when accurate, provides a shift in their sails to the potential winds of another perspective.[2] If they cannot change their perspective because they are flooded with sadness, anger, or frustration, they will not be able to learn from the wisdom of others to more effectively express their emotions.

If criticism is indeed accurate and warranted, parents and other authority figures must allow youth to recognize that acknowledging and changing behaviors is necessary and does not require significant opposition. If the child is allowed to feel sorry for themselves or cloud feedback with constant frustration or other strong emotions, they will not learn to make better life choices. Further, in a conflict, these children are not likely to acquire the critical knowledge of when they are wrong or be able to see that pattern in relationships. Both parties have to try to see the perspective of the other for a successful resolution. How many adult relationships become doomed because one side tries to prove they are right versus seeing things from the perspective of the other? Being right and being happy often are very different pathways.

Indicators Have Changed as to What Adulthood Looks Like from Childhood

Five life changes typically marked the transition from childhood to adulthood in the mid-twentieth century. The first was attaining and completing one's education. Then the second step was gaining a residence independently. Next was securing gainful employment, finally, (in previous generations) finding a partner and having children. These transitions are happening later and later for young adults (if at all).

As of 2016, 15 percent of twenty-five to thirty-five-year-old Millennials still lived in their parents' homes. This is five percentage points higher than the share of Generation Xers who lived in their parents' homes in 2000 when they were the same age (10 percent) and nearly double that of the Silent Generation who lived at home in 1964 (8 percent).[3]

Others Fight Your Battles, and You Never Learn How to Advocate for Yourself

What is the ultimate goal that parents, society, and teachers should have for the next generation? The objective is to prepare children for society to become productive, confident, and emotionally and physically healthy adults. If you never learn how to address conflict from others in the incubated world of childhood, you may be ill-prepared for adulthood.

However, how do children learn to advocate for themselves and strengthen those wings to fly confidently from the proverbial nest? It takes practice in uncomfortable and conflicted situations (within reason). This means that when sibling rivalry occurs (that is not physical) parents allow the children to find their way to solve this issue. It means that homework is not a "we" issue of parents being more responsible than the child but a "you" issue of the child knowing that this is the equivalent of an adult's job in their world.

If an adult always steps in to every disagreement, a child will never fully practice conflict resolution. According to many experts, 70 to 93 percent of communication is nonverbal, which can be challenging in reading for youth. Further, children who rely on communication via texting or social media are not practicing being literate in understanding these nonverbal cues that lead to or are involved in resolving of conflict.

Conflict teaches children to maintain emotional stability, express their feelings appropriately, and actively problem-solve. Without these abilities, children will likely have difficulty in the many emotionally heated situations they will experience ahead. Children who do not practice handling many natural conflicts that arise may become overly reactive and aggressively heated when exposed to them. Alternatively, the youth may become excessively passive and turn their anger inward and self-destructive. In either direction, they cannot fully appreciate or take responsibility for handling a conflict productively and independently.

Our Kids Can't Make Choices

How do we know our children are growing and maturing? When they begin to make decisions for themselves. Making sound choices in one's life is based on safety, one's ethics, and the individual morals of our society.[4] Problem-solving, whether in math or life, is based on practice, trial and error, and experience. If our children never have issues to solve independently, they simply will not have the aptitude for effectively evaluating future problems when they arise. This occurs when parents, society, or schools do not keep them from making age-appropriate choices nor holding them responsible for the choices that they make.

When children are not taught to make responsible choices, they will repeatedly tantrum, freeze, or make the wrong choice. Anxiety or anger is certainly not the place from which to analyze and evaluate making a sound decision. Yet, when our children do not build these skills, they regress to what is easiest and the most easily tapped emotionally (anger, anxiety, or depression). The problem? The choices made during these times only create a deeper hole from which to dig themselves out of.[5]

Job Responsibilities

When our children begin their first job in the workplace, they will have a specific listing of roles and responsibilities. Some of these roles may require them to do tasks they like more than others; however, they will be accountable for all parts of the job they are hired for. Without responsibility, they may pick and choose à la carte parts of the job they want to do and skip or skimp on the quality of the parts of the role they do not like.

If they have been raised not to have to do things they do not want to do, this type of selective behavior becomes acceptable. Working is about taking accountability for all aspects of the role (not just the items that you like to do). It also requires dialogue with a superior without standing behind a parent to be shielded from the barbs of taking responsibility.

5 What Can We Do as Parents to Grow Children's Responsibility?

Children Learn More from What You Do than What You Say

Many of our parents and grandparents have tried to impart their wisdom to us in our younger years. Stories often began with "When I was your age..." or "If I did that when I was young, they would..." These tales were intended to teach some vital life lessons that your elders had learned the hard way. The problem is that most of us, as children and adolescents, fail to see how this would apply to our lives or believe we somehow know better than we knew in the past generations. These diatribe of stories, lectures, and nagging failed to change our behavior as children. Likewise, it is reasonable to expect that telling these tales to our children will be met with a similar deaf ear.

Children, especially teenagers, watch what you do more than you say. If you tell them to take responsibility for their schoolwork and then blame your boss for missing a critical work deadline, they recognize this as a double standard. Behavioral modeling is more impactful to them than a 100 stories that you may tell. If you urge them to resolve a problem with a peer diplomatically and then curse out the cable customer service representative, they quickly recognize hypocrisy. Our youth learn more from what you do than what you say. Therefore, be sure that you are take an accurate accounting of your own strengths and weaknesses when taking responsibility for your actions. When you make a mistake, apologize and let them see how you resolve your errors responsibly. The answer "because I am the parent" holds little weight or respect in this regard.

Never Do for a Child What They Can Do for Themselves

Responsibility comes from action. In other words, children believe in themselves based on their competence in their abilities and those who trust them to do so. In nature, a bird cannot teach its chicks to fly by flying for them. The mother bird must stand by as the baby bird grows strength in its wings and trust that it can fly independently from the nest. Imagine the risk and tension of that chick flying for the first time and the danger of falling to the earth below.

As parents, we can stifle our children's ability to take responsibility when we continue to do for them what they should do safely for themselves. For instance, take making their bed. If we constantly come into their room and make their bed, they are not motivated to believe they can do it themselves. Additionally, if we continuously remake the bed after they do it, we are blatantly saying they cannot do an adequate job, so why bother?

Responsibility comes from a child learning to do independently what they are fully capable of. When we ask if the child can do it for themselves, we should ask if they are developmentally capable of doing the activity, if they can do it safely, and how this will be a learning experience to help them be independent and confident as an eventual adult.

We have several reasons for not allowing children to do things themselves. One of the primary reasons is simply a perceived lack of time, as it just takes too long to wait because of our frenzied adult routine. A secondary reason is that the child's ability does not meet our adult expectations of how the chosen activity should be "done right." Yet, we must ask ourselves if we are looking at our level of perfection or a "good enough" of what the child can do. A third, more subtle reason is that when our children grow independently, they are closer to our perception that they will not need us. In truth, our children can achieve emotional and physical independence, which is a healthy relationship, and they still need their parents. The primary and critical reason to not have? To not make our children dependent on us for their, or our, emotional happiness.

Make Certain You Are Naming the Right Emotion You Should Be Responsible For

If our children take responsibility for their emotions, they should know the emotion, or series of emotions, they are feeling. Emotions are rarely exclusively just one emotion. Instead, they are the complex blending and bleeding together of several emotions like watercolors on a canvas. Anger, for instance, often has elements of fear, frustration, sadness, or anxiety. Helping our children by talking with them and teasing out the other emotions they may also be feeling allows them to have a further handle and responsibility for their emotions.

Divorce Can Lead to Guilt

Divorce or separation is hard on families, especially children. Moving between two parents, navigating two different households and rules, and having two bedrooms and houses can be very stressful for children. This can lead one or both parents to be overly permissive and give a child everything they can want materially to make up for this perceived slight in the youth's childhood.

Sometimes, in this scenario, one parent is overly strict, and the other counterbalances this by being overly permissive, like the tipping scales of justice. This causes a child to have to deal with two extremes and creates confusion. Rules and parenting styles should be more balanced between authoritarian and permissive.

Initially, it may seem that trying to give our children everything out of love and guilt may be a good thing; however, relieving our guilt by spoiling our children does not teach them what they need to survive in the world. It is essential to recognize that divorce or separation is a sad and traumatic situation for the family unit but cannot not absolve either parent from teaching the child. The child must still follow the rules and earn rewards (versus be simply given things). Giving more material items or slacking on rules does not equate to showing more love or affection. Love and parenting must involve enforcing consistent, reasonable, and timely rules to teach them what they need to survive in the world regardless of situation.

The Belief of My Child Has the Right to Defend Themselves

Nothing is more challenging to see than our child being hurt. It often brings up our strongest parental instincts and emotions. The thought that our child is being victimized may lead parents to encourage their children to fight back in school against potential aggressors. The fact is, for better or worse, many schools institute zero-tolerance policies (or adhere to these informally) that do not allow for any form of physical violence (including self-defense). We may tell children that they have the right to defend themselves if they have no other choice, but school faculty should always be notified to intervene as a choice. That being said, all children are entitled to a safe school environment. However, this must rest on the education and administration addressing this issue versus vigilante justice and parents advocating to ensure this is enforced.

A few other elements also come into effect when considering fighting back against other children. Primarily, it is essential to recognize that, again, our children behave markedly differently in their relationships with peers. At times, both parties may share some responsibility in their interactions that, as parents, we may not be likely to know. In addition, in the case of physical altercations in society, both parties are often punished if both choose to use physical aggression to resolve a disagreement.

As parents, we may wish for the other child to be harshly punished for a perceived slight against our child. A question about the perceived aggressor is, would you provide the same advice to defend one of your children against their sibling as you would to a conflict with a peer? Alternatively, would the consequence you wish for that child who targeted your child be the same as the sanction for your child should they commit the identical behavior?

In generations past, bullying was considered a rite of passage. Some even falsely believed that this would somehow toughen up children. Now that society has seen the tragic results of bullying leading to depression, diminished self-esteem, and even suicide, most school policies have been strengthened much more tightly via state laws that have more severe consequences for bullies and school districts' enforcement of such laws. Parental ability to understand and navigate these rules with school administration adds teeth to addressing bullying and harassment issues in schools that were not as available previously in years past.

A Skewed View of Parental Responsibility

Parenting has never been as inundated with parental peer pressure as in our current society. Social media shows you "Facebook fables" of perfect families, with perfect children, doing perfect things. Children and parents will see advertisements geared to what they need to "keep up with the Joneses." Look around the holiday season, and you will see grown adults fighting over the last toy or video gaming system as though they were fighting for the last scrap of food in an apocalypse for the fear of their child going without the latest and greatest of something.

With all this peer pressures, it is no wonder that our modern generation has a skewed view of the role of parenting. We are always trying to do more and more—more activities, more things, more technology, and more stuff, and more, and more. The difficulty is that children and parents have develop a skewed vision of the role and responsibility of parents and what children feel they are entitled to.

Parents' job responsibilities are attained when they provide food, shelter, clothing, and, most significantly, love. Providing the latest technology, a car, or being the coolest parent on the block is not a part of responsible parenting. Yet, parents feel peer pressure to include the latter in their parenting inventory. In doing so, they forget that the items that are provided are attained without the child acknowledging the responsibility of earning them.

No Investment . . . No Understanding of Return

Let's take the above example a step further: a child gets a smartphone (these can range between $400 and $1,000), and they refuse to put a protective case on it because it will look ugly. Despite the parents imploring them of the cost of the investment and needing to protect it, they refuse to do so, and as a result, the smartphone screen is cracked when the child carelessly drops it on the floor. The parent states, "Do you know how much that phone costs? Why are you so careless?" The answer to that question is no. They do not understand how much the phone costs because they never took the responsibility of investing in it in the first place.

Therefore, now you have a child who believes they have no communication with their outside world and develops FOMO (a childhood term for Fear Of Missing Out in their social media world). The parent buys the child a new phone and tells them to "be more careful next time." Again, the child has no investment, responsibility, or consequence for their irresponsible previous behavior.

Hence, you must have some skin in the game if you want something. That is, the child must put some monetary or time investment into what they are doing or wanting (this can be in the form of chores or providing money from their allowance). Without this, they will not understand the responsibility of caring because they have no investment to care about. Without investment, there is simply little or no responsibility.

Integrity and Responsibility

The world has become such that, in many cases, children are rewarded for everything they do. Parents do not want their children to be left out or disappointed, so society has lauded them with empty praise. We now have participation and fourth-place awards and give an overabundance of praise for little or no achievement. When children are constantly given false and abstract praise such as "great job" or "you're such a great kid," we overinflate the child's ego without true merit or achievement. This is not to say that we should not praise children, but it should be a part of feedback for positive behavior versus for no reason at all.

Speaking of integrity requires our children to act within the beliefs, values, and morals we have taught them to adhere to. The issue is that children's integrity is often tested when no one is present. It occurs when they are out of the sight of their parents and need to make the right decision independently. Whether it be about peer pressure, cheating on an exam, or being offered drugs, these scenarios generally occur without a parent around. Additionally, they will not be overtly rewarded for doing the right thing at the time. There are no trophies for expressing your values. Sometimes, they will even receive retribution from peers whose suggestions they have rebuffed.

The concept of integrity is intertwined with the fabric of responsibility. Yet, how do we teach such a challenging concept to our children? First, like any aspect of the character, the familial demonstration of the trait of integrity is foremost. When no one else is watching our behavior, our children always are. This requires being a good model of actions versus uttering words of hypocrisy. Sometimes, integrity will confuse children who operate chiefly from an external egocentric dynamic until they mature, ideally, into empathic beings who embrace the concepts of morality and integrity. Hence, when you do something with responsibility and integrity, explain your rationale for how and why you acted the way you did in any particular scenario.

Additionally, set high values and expectations for your home and family regarding what is essential in behaving and reacting to others. This setting of expectations should be an ongoing dialogue in which all family members participate. In the case of organizations, they develop a mission statement that provides an overarching goal of how they expect to fit into the world's common good. A values statement written and visible to all family members provides a constant reminder of how decisions should be made and how one's family treats each other and those around them. Family values can further be classified into how we spend our money, handle jobs and school, what we do with our free time, and navigate ourselves as citizens of the digital world.

Reverse Chores

If we prepare children for accountability in society, we must teach them that everything done or not done in the community has a reciprocal price to pay. For instance, you pay for a cleaning service if you want your house cleaned but do not want to do it yourself. Don't want to mow your lawn? Let it go au naturel, or hire a landscaper. Don't want to do your laundry? That is fine, but if you have smelly, wrinkly clothes, take them to the dry cleaner.

The point is that society has a person or company for every job you do not want to do. The catch, of course, is that there is a financial cost based on the labor and how badly the customer wants the service completed. Similarly, if a child opts out of a chore or creates more work for another family member, they are responsible for paying for that service.

Let us say, for example, they leave their laundry in the washer and go out to spend time with their friends. Then, the family member who must complete the laundry service charges a fair market price. Another example is the child who comes to the parent and says they need an immediate ride to get supplies for a project or to a friend's house, they are charged, or barter services, because they are inconveniencing the other family member to act as an Uber driver suddenly. Services and inconveniences always cost money or labor to make another member's job easier.

Contracting for the Internet

How would you feel about a parent who allowed their child to socialize with a circle of adults that neither the parent nor child ever met? You would likely call that parent irresponsible at best and many other unflattering names at worst. Yet, this is the door we open when we allow our children access to the internet and social media. Statistics indicate that 17 percent of tweens have received messages or sent pictures that have made them feel uncomfortable online. An online predator has solicited one in seven children, while 32 percent of parents report allowing their children between seven and nine years of age to be on social media.[12]

As adults, we have two things that signify when we embark on a serious undertaking. The first is a test; if you are going to get a driver's license or a certification for many jobs, you must be trained and take a test. Secondly, suppose you enter into a significant undertaking. In that case, you sign a contract to recognize and agree to the gravity of your undertaking (whether it be a job, new car, or house). Similarly, for our children, becoming a citizen in the virtual world of the internet is a serious and potentially dangerous commitment. Thus, a written contract signifies they are entering one of the first solemn agreements in their young lives. An agreement where they do not just learn and agree to privileges but also understand the consequences of their actions.

All parties (parents, child, and a witness) should sign a contract. The contract should be easily visible and delineate clear rules and consequences.

Additionally, in developing the contract, the following should be considered by the parents:

- **Timeframe:** How much time is reasonable for them to use the internet? How will it be monitored, and when the time limit is reached, how will the internet sessions be ended? When are times that the internet can/cannot be used (such as at dinner or after bedtime)?
- **Behavior Online:** What are the expectations for online behavior that demonstrate safety and respect for themselves and others?
- **Monitoring:** How will the parent monitor internet communications and behavior (e.g., filters, devices in public areas, computer applications)?

- **Sharing:** What are the rules regarding what type of content shared on the internet is allowed and restricted?
- **Consequences:** What consequences will the parent impose if the child does not follow the rules appropriately?

As parents, we teach our children how to deal with strangers, cross the street safely, and behave when they meet new people. It is rare, however, to prepare the correct ways for our children to act on the World Wide Web. Having a child sign a contract agreement is insufficient to assure responsibility for themselves on the internet. We must educate them on how to be digital citizens of the internet community in the present era and how to be citizens of their actual neighborhoods.

To teach digital citizenship and responsibility requires that our children be able to understand and apply:

- How to use email, texting, and social media communications safely and appropriately before they try to do so.
- Understanding what gossip, rumors, and cyberbullying are involves recognizing them as online consequences and not using the internet as a forum for spreading these issues.
- Not sharing private information such as passwords, account information, names, and addresses.
- Don't use, or try to use, another person's account to access the internet.
- If you see anything inappropriate or feel uncomfortable, immediately stop and contact your parents.
- Have permission from your parent(s) before you buy anything online.
- Know when to stop using the internet and social media.
- Don't believe everything you see online; some statements are not credible, and others are blatantly false.

Facebook Fables

Before making their first post, many children on social media have already demonstrated a lack of responsibility and a tendency to be deceitful at the most basic level. How is that possible? The first question about the social media platform contract is requesting your age. If you are under the required age (usually between thirteen and eighteen), in theory, you should be restricted from the social media site due to content and conversation that may not be appropriate for one's age.

What is the gatekeeper for getting on these social media sites? Does it require you to gain parental permission, show your birth certificate, or provide a notarized letter documenting your age? No, it is simply a prompt on the site that requires you certify you are over the above-stated age required to be on the social media site. Hence, children must lie about their age to even get on most social media sites.[3] According to research, one in every three children has lied to get on one or more social media sites. Most research for children designates those thirteen and above only because this is when children are technically supposed to be able to access social media. Along this path, the average for this grouping of thirteen-year-olds is 5.8 hours daily on social media.[4]

If you lie about your age, it is possible that those on the internet can lie about other details regarding essential traits. You can alter your account name, your gender, your account photo, and your education. In short, you can shift any aspect of yourself to what you want others to see. The farther one's account details are from who they are, the further they can also distance themselves from the responsibility of their actions on that respective social media account and your actions. In short, you can play a role and a script that differs from who you actually are.

The "Not My Child" Syndrome of Parenting

Have you ever had the experience when you were younger of your parents being on a tirade of disciplining you or your siblings, yelling, screaming, seemingly out of control, and then the phone rings? That parent, who previously seemed out of control, changes their voice and demeanor to the so-called "telephone voice." The voice is warm, pleasant, and patient. What happened? How did that parent shift direction so quickly?

We all change our personality, attitude, and tone depending on the situation. We recognize that specific environments, such as our jobs and peers, require us to be more reserved and professional. Other environments, such as parties, may require us to be more open and uninhibited. Yet, in another environment, we may be convinced to do things that we may not usually do based on the comfort level of those we are with and our mood.

Another example is when we are with our significant other or our children. You may say things to them, both positive and negative, that you would likely never say to a stranger or a co-worker acquaintance. Why? You have a comfort level that lets you put your hair down and say everything you want versus carefully constructing your words with those you don't know quite as well.

The point is that children also act differently when they are not around you, and we must be aware of that. To say "not my child" is to dismiss the role of peer pressure and the changing faces that all of us (children included) use to navigate the world. We often think, however, that the behavior our children exhibit is a direct reflection of us. This guilt and self-shaming thus place the blame for our children's reckless or poor behavior on ourselves and deflect from their responsibility. This strengthens our defensiveness and doubting what others (in many cases adults) are telling us about our own child's behavior.

Can children be "picked on" by teachers, coaches, and other authority figures? Of course, however, when you hear the same statement more than once about what your child does, and you ignore it or defend it, you and your child cannot solve the problem. The problem persists because you refuse to recognize it as one. Mistakes children make are opportunities to learn because learning for many children comes from these very experiences of making mistakes.

How many of us have heard the stories of our parents walking barefoot both ways to school in a snowstorm and all of the hardships they endured as children? Many of us, as children ourselves, have rolled our eyes and failed to learn anything from these stories. Most of us learn through a combination of parental influence, trial and error, and the consequences of our actions. When we are shielded from any of these, we fail to understand.

An Unlimited Bank Account Financial Responsibility

If you ask a child about credit cards or an ATM, they will often tell you when you run out of money, you simply go to one of those two sources for more money. They frequently fail to understand that credit cards or ATMs are not an endless wishing well for which springs money. How many adults do you know who see those same credit cards as a source of infinite revenue and fail to understand the responsibility of paying those debts back and are blinded to the enormous amounts of interest accruing?

Children learn the concept of money when given a junior example of how money works in the real world. Getting money for what one does to contribute to others shows that money is earned and not just simply provided in a seemingly limitless supply. Additionally, earning gives an understanding of the actual value of money. How would we know that is so? Children will often purchase items extravagantly when the parent is responsible for paying. However, they will think twice when the limited monetary funds come out of their pocket.

The issue when a child begins to earn allowance is that they see their labor as valuable to their family. Therefore, they try to negotiate a monetary reimbursement for everything they do. Although their craftiness in this area is natural, children must learn that their role within a family unit means responsibilities that must be completed outside of simple, constant monetary compensation. Therefore, how do we teach mutual responsibility financially and the obligations of being a member of their family?

Consider a commission-based allowance system. First, determine the responsibilities your child should have as a family member. They will not be paid for these tasks because, just as if you might cook or carpool them, they are part of your expected responsibilities as a family member. Next, decide which chores are commission-based and the payment they will receive for each job.

This has many benefits over traditional allowances. First, the child recognizes that they have voluntary obligations to others and their activities to earn money (much as in the adult world). Second, they know how much they will get paid for their jobs and that the more strenuous a job is, the greater the reward there will be. Finally, it may encourage working harder if saving up for an item, which teaches monetary self-discipline.

Of course, financial well-being should not be used merely for selfish ends. Our children can and should learn how to donate and be charitable to the many who are less well off. This can be done by volunteering their time with charitable/nonprofit organizations with the family or donating a portion of their money regularly. To be meaningful, children need to know precisely what their money or time will help, and a family discussion of charity and being cognizant of others who have less than themselves should be addressed each time money or volunteer time is given.

Children Can Be Seen and Heard

In 1450, a clergyman wrote and published a book called *Mirk's Festival*, in which he stated that "Children should be seen and not heard." The reference referred to the fact that children do not know to be a part of adult conversation and should thus be ignored. Almost 600 years later, we are still familiar with this statement, and some might agree with it today.[5]

How do children learn conflict resolution, problem-solving, and empathy if they are not heard? As parents, our role is to prepare them at ever younger ages for what society has in store for them when they become adults. Therefore, instead of "being seen and not heard," a more apt statement for today may very well be "every child gets their say, but not always their way." We allow children to give viewpoints and opinions in conflict to practice these skills. They, as children, do not have the same level of experience or wisdom, so their opinion may not be given the same weight as an adult. However, they play an active role in offering solutions to problems they encounter. This helps them to see that there are many opposing views and sharpens their ways to solve an issue (versus just their one viewpoint).

Don't Always Assume Your Child Knows What They Are Responsible For

For our children to know what they should be responsible for, we must be clear in our communication and delegation. First, explain what they must do in clear, manageable steps. When explaining what they should do, it must be direct about what you want them to do versus telling them simply what not to do. If they hear you saying the words *do not* more than the word *do* you are assuming that the child knows what *to do*. The word "don't" restricts information and is not productive in telling a child (or anyone) what you want them *to do*. In short, use the word *do* more than *do not* when delegating responsibilities.

Next, monitoring what the child is doing by telling them what they are doing correctly is essential. When giving feedback, be sure it is behaviorally specific. This means that instead of vague statements like "good job" or "you are a good boy/girl," clarify which behaviors indicate they are doing the task correctly. It is critical to give positive feedback and let go of the fact that well-intentioned actions may not be to your specific abilities or aptitude. If you have several steps or activities you want to be done, teach them priorities of what steps are more critical to complete before others.

Separate Behavior from the Child

It can damage a child's self-esteem and subsequent ability to take responsibility if they believe their mistakes make them inherently flawed. Yes, we all make mistakes, but the behaviors often reflect errors and poor choices versus who we are as a whole person. If we come to harbor only on errors, children begin to believe that their mistakes define who they are.

How do we prevent the child from engaging in this behavior? This can be done by first avoiding comments that are global labels such as: "stop being a crybaby, you are being bad, why can't you be more like your brother/sister, your little brother/sister even knows better." Instead, be specific in focusing on the behavior they are engaging in, the alternative behavior you wish them to conduct, and the potential consequence should they not do so. For example, "I see you are being mean to your sister, and you know we are kind to each other in our family. Go upstairs and take fifteen minutes to think about your behavior, and I want you to return with a sincere apology." Thus, focusing on the behavior and the consequence versus the child as a whole avoids the implication that the child's somehow essentially deficient and spares their self-esteem.

Our Children Are Special but No More Special than Another

As parents, we are responsible for teaching our children how to be responsible members of society. This means that when they enter the world of school or society, they must recognize that they are a part of the community around which they revolve (not vice versa). When our children are toddlers, they are egocentric; that is, the world, and everyone in it, revolves around them. As they mature, they should realize that the world does not revolve around them, and they are responsible for interacting and compromising with others. Ideally, they learn that self-esteem is not the same as self-centeredness and are responsible for themselves as well as their behavior outside their home.

As parents, our children are often the center of our world, and we see them for the exceptional individuals that they are. This is important and necessary in building our child's self-worth and in our special relationship, each of us forges with our children. The danger becomes when we overvalue our children in society. You may ask how it is possible I can overthink the value of my child?

Overvaluing one's child is when, as a parent, we tend to consider our child as more unique and deserving than that of others. In society, in theory, we all start as equal; you may work to get something you deserve, but you are not more special than anyone else. When we do not balance a child's values with their peers, they often find themselves feeling alone and isolated. This can create a child, according to research, who is narcissistic and does not see responsibility to anyone but themselves.[6]

We must balance our child's self-esteem with a healthy dose of empathy, tolerance, and recognition of the wants and needs of others. This comes from monitoring playdates and having your child voice how another may feel (versus feelings being thought of as a one way street). They must realize they are important and unique but no more, or less important, than any other child. To give them the message that their "specialness" makes them better than someone else sets the tone for narcissistic behavior and a world of disappointment ahead.[7] A narcissistic child will see everything that happens positive as 100 percent because of what they did and anything negative as 100 percent the fault of outside factors. Thus, they never recognize how to change behavior to solve problems independently.

So, how do we raise a confident and self-assured child without the risk of being narcissistic and irresponsible to the concerns of peers or others? The first aspect is offering a balanced understanding of your child's abilities. That is, your child, like every other human on the planet, has many strengths, abilities, and weaknesses. Be realistic about this and recognize that each personality type and child comes with their own unique set of strengths and drawbacks.

For instance, a child who is introverted in our extrovert-dominated society tends also to be more creative, cautious, and self-reflective.[8,9]

Along the same lines, the opposite effect may be created if you give your child exaggerated or inflated praise (hoping that more praise equals more self-esteem). Research supports that when a parent provides overly inflated, overly optimistic, empty praise, a child's self-esteem decreases. Why? Data suggests two probable causes: (1) Because a parent is subtly setting a standard that a child feels they can never attain, or (2) The child begins to believe these overly inflated views of themselves and develops overly self-centered traits that are an attempt at overcompensating for low self-esteem.[10]

Parental-encouraged competition can also be a double-edged sword. It can motivate a child to be the best they can be, be responsible for their actions, and discipline themselves. Alternatively, it can teach them to do everything to step on the heads of others on the way up the ladder of sports or academics and not care about being responsible for other's feelings or needs. When a parent encourages competition against others, it can create the same responsibility and superiority to self, which we find in self-obsessed and conceited behavior. Further, these same children believe they should be superior to other groups, students, or people, leading to discrimination or bullying.

Instead, when a parent encourages temporal comparison (contrasting if one's current self is improving/declining than one's past self or behavior) it becomes a much better indicator. It encourages children to be responsible for their well-being and "the best me they can be." While social comparison teaches a child to try to be better than others. Temporal comparison further fosters self-improvement, a sense of improvement, pride, and responsibility for oneself.[11]

How Children Learn Prejudice and Tolerance for Those Who Are Different from Themselves

As we discussed earlier, those children who are encouraged to utilize social comparison (being better than others) can fall into the trap of thinking they are better than other groups of people who are different from them. That being said, how, as parents, do we create children that are responsible and tolerant of persons who are both the same and different from us? It is important to realize first that all of us have known and unknown biases that are partially shaped by what we are told by our parents, family members, friends, and society itself. In fact as early as preschool children may already be demonstrating a preference to select friends of the same race.[12]

So how do parents teach all members of society to be tolerant and responsible? First, by opening the conversation with our children about the concept of race and that racism does exist. The most impactful way to teach our children about diversity is to have them experience other cultures. This can be through food, seeing new cultures, traveling, and looking at problems from a diverse point of view. Research has shown that this notion, called cultural socialization, is the most effective way to teach responsibility and understanding of those different from yourself.[13]

Another aspect is what the parents say and do regarding their prejudices. As we noted previously, children learn much more from their parents in what they do and say, which teaches prejudice directly and subtly through what they do and the reinforcement method. The most impactful way children learn from their parents' prejudiced attitudes is by observing how their parents talk and interact with people from different groups.

When You Are Afraid, or Your Child Is Afraid

Anxiety has become an epidemic in the last several decades for adults and children alike. In particular, child anxiety has grown exponentially to the point that modern children show more anxiety than the average childhood psychiatric patient of the 1950s had experienced.[14] This may make us as parents want to eliminate as much anxiety from our children's worlds as possible. Alternatively, with our anxiety about the dangerous world outside of our door, we may want to lock our children inside the doors of our homes and never let them out.

Neither way solves any issues, unfortunately, and ultimately, our children must be responsible for their behaviors and anxiety. When we try to take away their anxieties, what we find is that it creates more anxiety because they believe they are ill-equipped to handle their problems and must always rely on others to survive and grow. Keeping our children away from the responsibility of their anxieties only creates confirmation that all of the fears they are feeling are justified and makes those mountains even harder to climb.

So, how do we help our children take responsibility for their anxiety? The first step is to allow them to acknowledge that we all have anxiety. Let your child(ren) know that you have had anxiety and how you have overcome those hurdles. Next, let your child know how to identify their anxiety and worrisome thoughts. How do you do this? By recognizing our anxious thoughts with the simple words in our head, "What if?" What if are the future-focused words that generally begin each of us down a cascading cycle of anxiety. "What if I fail at this project . . . what if I never get another job . . . what if I lose my home . . . what if I end up homeless?" This cycle occurs quickly and rapidly to a worst-case scenario basis.

Additionally, set aside a few minutes each day in which your child can discuss their worries and what their worst-case scenarios are and have them come up with strategies with you that they can utilize to address their anxieties and worries independently. Doing so will help them learn to discipline their anxiety and take responsibility for coming up with solutions on their own.

How We Inadvertently Allow Children to Shift Responsibility to Adults

Sometimes, our children will say, "You don't love me, you hate me, I am a failure, I have no friends!" This can be when they have gotten in trouble, disappointed you, or are just feeling sorry for themselves about something they had done or has been done to them. The answer many parents and other adults provide is to reassure the child with statements such as, "Of course we love you, you are wonderful, and you are successful at . . . (Insert example)." The problem is that the child then always looks external to themselves for validation, emotional regulation, and approval.

What happens the next time, or many times, that the child has an issue with taking responsibility for their self-esteem or soothing their emotions? They will again look externally to themselves and do so repeatedly. Whether it be a teacher, a parent, or another adult, they constantly and consistently look to others to fill the vacuum for their waning self-esteem and never see it as something they can repair. As they age, it becomes friends, girlfriends, boyfriends, or others that they look to fill that void of self-belief.

So what do we do as parents to plug that leaking hole that constantly deflates the bubble of our child's self-esteem? Instead of giving them constant words of self assurance that temporarily fills their void. Ask them to think of three things that I love about you (when they say you do not love me), name three of your friends (when they say they have no friends), or name three things you are good at (when they say they are a failure). In doing so, you encourage them to independently develop self-esteem versus always seeking reassurance outside themselves.

Anger Is an Acceptable Emotion . . . But You Must Take Responsibility for That, Too

Many children think anger is not an acceptable emotion. Often, this is because they associate rage, a behavior that can be wildly destructive, either verbally or physically. Yet, anger can be an emotion that helps children stand up for themselves and, under the right circumstances, can provide the energy to drive a child toward changing something they do not like. Without anger, a child may become overly passive and permissive. In other words, they become a virtual doormat for others and risk being influenced or bullied by more dominant peers.

What is not acceptable, however, is when a child throws a tantrum, stamps their feet, and then leaves parents or others responsible for guessing what they are upset about. In doing so, they fail to assert what they need and what upsets them. This shifts the responsibility of others to determine their emotional state via mind reading or guessing. Again, it takes the responsibility for the child's emotions off the youth and toward others.

When a child is angered, they need to do three things to help solve a problem (such as being angry). These are contained in three components of their message (see Table 5.1).

Table 5.1 is known as "I" Messages and is used for children and adults in many counseling situations. The benefits of "I" Messages include a clearer understanding of the person's feelings, not making others feel blamed and defensive or reactive, and providing a positive means for problem-solving.

Utilizing this format also helps children realize that they have to offer solutions versus further problems when they come to their parents for an

Table 5.1 A Model for Asserting Responsibility in Conflict

Words	Message
"I feel _____"	Voice the emotion they feel (with the knowledge they may have more than one feeling).
"Because _____"	What is the situation from their perspective?
"So I need _____."	What it is that they believe they need to resolve this situation appropriately?

answer. Doing so also parallels what will be expected of them in the so-called "real world," in which the expectation is to come to your supervisor with prospective solutions for an issue rather than pointing out a constant stream of problems or obstacles.

Tattling, Telling, and Parental Responsibility in Both

As parents, we never want to see our children hurt in any way, and it can bring out the mama or papa bear in any of us. We cannot fight all of our children's battles and issues, or we risk crippling them as they grow to be able to handle themselves when we are not around. So how do we and our children know when we should step in or step out and let the child handle an issue independently? When do we risk the labeling of our child as a "snitch" or "tattle tale," and when do we step in as responsible parents?

The answer is to classify issues for our children regarding when they should defer topics to us and try to handle problems themselves. In short, issues that can create a danger for themselves or others should be channeled to parents or other trusted authority figures. They can attempt to handle most other matters independently and be responsible for their actions accordingly.

Here are some examples of which problems fall into each category (see Table 5.2):

With these minor problems, discussing how to address issues with the child is permissible. A good inventory of potential choices are those that are used in the Kelso's Choice Curriculum.[15] These include teaching your child the following: talking it out with a peer, taking turns and sharing, ignoring the

Table 5.2 Distinguishing and Dividing Responsibility

Larger Issues	Smaller Issues
Bullying–This can create potential physical or emotional damage to the child.	Cutting in line- No issues of safety to note.
Being told to keep a secret-Unless it is a party or gift these are often kept from parents because they are something a parent would not condone if they knew about it.	Sibling rivalry issues- Squabbles should try to be solved independently unless they could potentially become physical.
Drugs or alcohol: Obviously, issues of drugs and alcohol become concerning at any age and represent dangerous behavior.	Disagreements with friends during a play date: Disagreements are natural in any relationship and are good practice for developing conflict resolution skills.
Being "dared" to do something: "Dares," like secrets, create an issue of a child being told to intentionally violate a social norm or parental rule.	Child-Student School Work Issues: No one is getting hurt in this issue, and your child's work and homework are their responsibility for completing or explaining why they did not do so to their teacher.
Fear: If a child is excessively fearful of something, this could represent a danger that they may or may not be aware of.	Not Sharing- Children must learn how to compromise independently of their parents (unless the issue becomes physical).

issue at hand, walking away from a problem, telling the other child to stop, finding another activity to go to, or giving themselves a time-out to cool down until they can make a more rational decision. It is important to note that more than one of these choices may need to be implemented before finding the correct one that fits the situation.

Bullying and School Responsibility

Bullying can be a cancer that quickly erodes the school climate. Like cancer, bullying needs an optimal environment to metastasize. It requires a bully, a target, and the less-mentioned bystanders. Bystanders are the equation that can tip the scales, yet bystanders often think they have the least responsibility in that formula.

What happens when adults act as bystanders and hesitate to take responsibility and get involved? Enter the tragic story of Kitty Genovese. On March 28, 1964, Kitty returned from her bartender job in the morning's wee hours. She was attacked, beaten, and raped. During this time, it was reported that many people had opened windows in the Queens, New York, apartment complex and likely heard her cries for help. Despite her begging, no one helped or even called the police. This lack of others taking the responsibility to get involved became later known as "The Kitty Genovese Effect."[16] It highlights that when social groups exist, they may tend to do less than as individuals (known as social loafing) and the bystander effect may cause people in a group to become paralyzed in decision-making due to awaiting someone else to jump in.

If schools train students to stand up and take responsibility for their school society and climate, we change the dynamic of responsibility back to the student body. Seventy percent of students report witnessing bullying in their schools. Unfortunately, bystanders only get involved in bullying a mere 20 percent of the time. However, 60 percent of bullying situations cease when a bystander intercedes. Further, when asking the educational community of students, 57 percent of them said that they believe peer interventions are effective.[17]

Yelling, Emotions, and Reaction Will Never Teach Responsibility

If you had parents who were overly reactive and yelled, screamed, or berated you when you made a mistake, you likely are fearful of your parents. The issue is that children become afraid of their parents with this form of parenting. A healthy level of respect is essential in parenting. However, fear creates unwanted consequences. For instance, when a parent is overly emotional or reactive to a child, that child learns to be shamed for mistakes they make. Furthermore, the child will do almost anything to avoid creating a volcano of anger in their parents, including lying, omitting information, or avoiding controversial discussions with their parents at all costs.

In contrast, look at how consequences are applied in the so-called "real world?" With little emotion and words. You are pulled over for speeding, and the police officer says, "License and registration, please." They should not continue screaming and yelling at you for your reckless behavior. It is not professional, nor does it provide you the self-respect that we all deserve as human beings.

Hence, giving a consequence with as little emotion and words as possible teaches our children how the consequences of not taking responsibility for their actions are handled in the real world. They are provided with little fanfare, words, or emotions. If you choose to speed, you pay a fine. If you decide not to pay your electric bill, your electricity is shut off. Responsibility is tied to consequences but not to emotions or ridicule.

No Empty Apologies . . .

When our children say sorry, it can become a knee-jerk reaction. That is, they simply say the words just because it is an expectation to do so. Ask them what they are sorry for, but they cannot explain why. An empty apology is no apology at all.

What do you do when you apologize? You explain why you are sorry, and most of us try to offer some kind of reparation. When your child offers an apology, work together with them on a way to provide that retribution. It could be writing a note, paying for something they damaged, or confronting the lie they told by apologizing directly to that person. It could even be a monetary retribution. The most important question is how we can make this an educational lesson they can apply to when they wrong someone in society down the road later.

Warnings and Threats Do Not Teach Responsibility (Usually)

If you are going to give a consequence, do it. Threatening or going on long tirades about what you will do does not teach children responsibility for their behavior. In addition, warning children of a consequence for blatantly wrong behavior teaches them they get "a free shot or two" before we implement a consequence.

For instance, your son hauls off and hits his younger sister; you provide a warning not to do that again. What you are implying is that he did not know that hitting his sister was wrong, and so you are trying to teach alternative correct behavior. If the behavior is flagrantly wrong, the child need not be warned of the consequences.

What Are Consequences, Punishments, and Discipline?

Often, we confuse the terms consequences, punishment, and discipline in parenting. Yet, these are all very different interventions and create very different results. Punishing a child is often done out of our energy and emotion. If we are tired or angered, we are more likely to give a harsh punishment. Punishment is frequently used to create shame and blame the child for their behavior without any real connection to what they did. Punishment creates resentment, anger, and fear. It does not teach taking responsibility and understanding one's actions from an educational framework.

Discipline has the differing goal of teaching something to the child. For instance, when we go to college or start a career, it is to learn a discipline. A discipline is meant to teach and provide something valuable to the individual or society. It is not reactive, but proactive, to understand what you need to do in the future and does not negatively influence the parent-child relationship. It is taught to teach versus punishment and a demand to simply obey whatever is said.

What is our ultimate goal as parents and caretakers of the next generation? It is not to teach them to be children forever and depend on us. The fact of the matter is that, unfortunately, we will be gone one day, and they must be able to be responsible for every component of their lives (and probably the lives of their own family). Therefore, the time begins to tick when our children are out of the womb, and we need to get them ready for that monumental goal of independence and responsibility.

How do we then decide the consequences for our children? Make every consequence that you employ an educational experience. This means asking yourself how the result I am providing will teach them what they can expect in society and when they leave the comfort of our nest. If you cannot think of a natural or logical consequence, ask yourself if you had committed a similar indiscretion as your child had done, what would society, your job, and/or your family and friends provide for you in the way of a consequence? Next, think of how you can dilute that consequence so that your child will understand the concept of the consequence when they enter the real world of society.

These logical or natural consequences are sometimes easy to establish. For instance, if your child refuses to eat what you have made for dinner, you have two obvious choices: make another meal for them or not make anything else (forcing them to eat what you made). Some parents will feel bad and make another alternative meal, while others will offer nothing.

What do you do? Think of what this scenario will look like when they are independent young adults. As an adult, if you look in your pantry and have limited ingredients, you can cook what you can afford. If not, the natural consequence is that you will have to choose to go hungry. Later, if you are still hungry, you will eat what you have in the pantry or continue to be hungry. This is how the real world operates.

The 3 R's are a good guide for effectively using logical and natural consequences with our children.

- **Related:** Is the consequence you provide directly related to the behavior? Again, think if you had done a similar behavior, is your consequence mimicking, in some way, what you are providing to the child?
- **Respectful:** Is the consequence you are demonstrating respect to the child in that you are not using it to blame or make the child feel shame? Hence, are you teaching rather than punishing just for the sake of punishment and proving your superiority as a parent?
- **Reasonable:** Is the consequence reasonable for the infraction, or are you just punishing the child? Is it age-appropriate and possible to enforce, and does it teach the child the proper lesson within a given timeframe and manner they will understand? Or are you just threatening and incapable of doing what you say you will do?

Other examples of real-world logical and natural consequences are listed in Table 5.3

Table 5.3 Examples of Natural and Logical Consequences

Problem/Issue	Real-World Natural and Logical Consequences
Your child is rude to their peers.	Their peers don't play or spend time with them until your child alters and learns better social skills.
Your child chooses not to bathe daily or take care of their hygiene.	Their peers will tell them that they smell or criticize their hygiene until they take care of these issues.
Your child doesn't do their homework.	They will have to explain to their teacher why they failed to complete their responsibility.
Your child lies.	They must apologize directly to who they lied to.
Your child does not put clothes in the hamper to be washed.	They will have limited clean clothes to wear the next day.
Your child doesn't do your chores in a timely fashion.	The parent chooses when they will do their chores at some inopportune time for the child.
Your child makes a mess.	Your child cleans it up before moving on to any other recreational activity.
Your child has a tantrum in public.	You are immediately removed from the situation.
Your child does not put a protective case on their tablet.	They will have to put up with having a cracked screen until they have earned the money to fix it.
Your child stays up late and does not follow the bedtime schedule.	Your child gets up still on time and is tired the next day.

Corporal Punishment and Trying to Force Responsibility

Sometimes we hear about the so-called "good old days" in which children listened more effectively because they were given a swat on the butt if they did not listen. In those days when the child would cry and have tantrums, the parental response may well be, "I'll give you something to cry about!"

However, the question is whether corporal punishment is a more effective means of teaching a change in behavior or responsibility.

First, corporal punishment often sends a mixed message. For instance, if I spank a child for hitting their little brother, am I not displaying the very same behavior that I am ridiculing my child for? It also teaches the child that violence is an acceptable aspect of parent-child, or any, relationships in which one does not obey another's rules or restrictions. What does this say for when our children have their future relationships? Additionally, if corporal punishment escalates, it can go over the line between spanking and outright abuse.

What does the research say regarding the usage of corporal punishment and its efficacy? Researchers have found that spanking may elevate a child's aggression levels as well as decrease the overall quality of the parent-child relationship. Numerous research projects have found that parents do not use spanking as a consistent punishment. Instead, they are more likely to use it when angered or upset. In fact, in a survey, 44 percent of parents reported that they used spanking about half the time when they were emotionally spent and just lost their patience.[18] Much as if we talked about punishment earlier, corporal punishment is done out of energy and emotion versus teaching responsibility or for some educational purpose.

Fairness and Responsibility

Younger children tend to have a very concrete view of fairness. To be fair, everyone should get the same thing and be treated equally. As adults, we sometimes inadvertently reinforce this belief when we give awards or accolades to all participants for simply competing in some activity. The problem is that the world is not one where everyone is treated equally; politics, connections, and those with other talents will get things over your child and every other child.

Fairness, from a more realistic perspective, means everyone gets what they need. It does not, unfortunately, necessarily mean we always get what we want. It suggests we should be responsible for our behaviors and try our best. Being fair to others also conveys being accountable and compassionate, and helping others around you who cannot provide you anything in return. As discussed earlier, children may see fairness as a lateral relationship of equal give and take. This means that those peers who cannot give them something are of little or no use. We must teach compassion as a part of fairness or what is better known as social justice (the viewpoint that everyone deserves to be treated fairly and advocated for accordingly).

As discussed earlier, teaching social justice means exposing our children to diversity. It also means talking to our youth about the news and, when aspects of social justice come up, having a productive and insightful discussion. Having our children volunteer with us for charitable causes is another way they can understand charitable giving and see inequalities firsthand that they would otherwise not understand nor be exposed to.

Parental Anxiety Is Contagious

When parents consistently overprotect their children, they do so from a place of both anxiety and fear of what could happen to them. Children rely on their parents to be the rock of their stability, so they become even more afraid and nervous when their parents are fearful and anxious. It is necessary for parents to not only worry about what can happen if a child does something new but also to be concerned about what they will miss if they do not do something. If one watches the news, it is easy to become increasingly paranoid about the world as being more dangerous than it is. That is not to say that our society is entirely safe and harmless; we must develop an accurate and unskewed view of our surroundings.

More about Parents and Technology Responsibility

When you ask many parents about their responsibility in their children's access to or use of technology a common response is, "My child knows more about technology then I do." Often, this response is followed by a proverbial throwing up of one's hands and giving up. Unfortunately, this does nothing for helping protect children from the dangers that lie in the dark alleys of the internet.

Parents don't need a master's degree in cybersecurity to protect their children. Fortunately, many programs and applications exist to do that for them. Here are some twrms that parents should know to responsibly protect children:

- Filters: Installing technology filters can allow parents to develop limits on the content that a child can handle responsibly.
- Accounts: A simple search of videos will allow parents to step-by-step block social media account access to inappropriate information that the parent does not wish their child to view.
- Develop a family media plan: We often allow technology into our home without any proactive thought of a comprehensive plan. Develop a strategy that all family members agree upon in terms of type of internet access, content viewable, and amount of time.

Bigger Children, Bigger Risks, Bigger Responsibilities

As children grow, it is common sense that they will outgrow their clothing; before you know it, you will need to purchase new clothing. It should also seem common logic that as children grow developmentally, parents must change their expectations and responsibilities for the child they have outgrown. When we do not do this, we stifle our children's growing maturity and our expectations of them.

What do growing responsibilities and your child's maturity look like? As young as toddlers, they can begin to put away the things they take out to play with and clean up small messes they have made. As they progress to preschool age, they should start bringing their dishes to the sink, making their bed (to the best of their ability), and dividing laundry by what is white and what is colored. At school age, it is appropriate for them to vacuum, help put away the groceries, put the dishes in the dishwasher, and help make dinner and fold laundry. By adolescence, they should be able to do almost all these activities independently.

As children grow in responsibilities, so do they grow in privileges they should be able to enjoy. For instance, bedtime is an example of how maturity and responsibility earn more privilege for a child. According to the National Sleep Foundation, a preschooler should get ten to thirteen hours per night of sleep; at school age, this shifts to nine to eleven, and finally, in adolescence, to eight to ten hours.[19] This allows a guideline for children to recognize that as they grow, they are given more freedom within limits. Another example is curfews, in which older children can stay out longer. Parents decide these jointly with their children based on the maturity and well-being of the child.

The "I Don't Care" Child and Responsibility

Parents often find it challenging to deal with children who do not care much about anything. The rote response to anything the parent says or asks is answered with a resounding, "Well, I don't care!" So, how does a parent muster responsibility from a kid who does not seem to care about anything or any interventions they may try? In other words, if a child does not care, how will we get them to take responsibility for anything they do?

First, suppose a child truly cares about nothing, and we cannot find anything to motivate them. In that case, the parent should strongly consider getting that child evaluated for depressive issues. The Mayo Clinic defines clinical depression by symptoms such as a profound loss of interest or pleasure in most or all normal activities, such as hobbies or sports.[20] It is essential that if your child truly cares about nothing and cannot seem to be motivated by any intrinsic rewards or motivation, what the cause of this depressed state may be. A child who does not care about anything is rarely emotional because they simply do not, or cannot, care about whatever is around them and should be immediately evaluated by a mental health professional.

Looking at emotion and body language versus what your child says is essential. Let me give an example. For instance, if your seventeen-year-old teen does not complete the chores they are scheduled to do and they come bounding down the stairs to go out with their boyfriend/girlfriend for the evening, and you say you cannot have the car tonight, what would their response be? It may very well be, "I don't care!" This may be preceded by throwing down the car keys and running back upstairs in a mini tantrum. Their *words* indicate not caring. However, their *emotions and reactions* indicate the very opposite reaction. They show they care via their emotions and reactivity, which is the actual language of their feelings. The contrary words they state are the opposite for an excellent reason.

If you know their emotional cards as the authority figure, you will win the game every time. In other words, if you know the most effective and impactful consequences for your children, you will logically employ them each time. On the flip side, if you do not see what works as consequences, you will be unable to apply practical solutions for disciplining and restricting the things most important to the child. Therefore, the parent will throw their hands up in desperation because nothing seems to work to teach the child about limits or consequences.

Parents and Peer Pressure

When you hear the words "peer pressure" the immediate thought is children or adolescents. We think of this pressure in relation to drugs, alcohol, or being dared to do something. Peer pressure does not end with the stress and strain of childhood. Rather, peer pressure extends to adulthood, one's neighborhood, and office politics.

As a result of peer pressure a certain amount of societal homeostasis exists. When everyone is doing, or not doing, something pressure exists to follow the path most traveled. With social media this trend is even more cemented because you can see video and dialogue of your neighbors in a way never before exploited in previous generations.

This means we, and our children, often follow the manner of what others do and find acceptable. If all the children in the neighborhood have smartphones, my child must have one. If all the children are allowed to do something my kids should too. If you go against the tide of what is the norm, pressure is exerted from all sides: from the other parents, your kids, and even the media.

Peer pressure is not always negative. In cases of children, peers, with the right influence, can group together to encourage socially positive behavior. Paralleling this, parents with the same views and parenting beliefs can cluster together to support each other's philosophies on parenting.

The premise of support groups is to assist others with similar beliefs or problems. Parents certainly have a job cut out for them as no manual exists. Support, ideas, and not feeling you are alone are vital in survival in a rapidly changing and frenetic world.

6 A Responsible School
Public Education in Schools

Education Has Changed a Great Deal over the Years, and So Have Responsibilities

In the 1830s, Horace Mann, Massachusetts's Secretary of Education, established common schools. These schools provided all youth with free public education funded by the state. The primary goal of these schools was to teach the 3 R's of reading, writing, and arithmetic, along with history, geography, and grammar. Additionally, civic virtues were addressed; however, the primary goal was academics.[1]

Two hundred years later, schools teach many subjects outside of traditional academics. Public schools now have a curriculum that includes social-emotional learning, character education, and how to deal with technology in the form of digital citizenship.

These topics must be taught alongside the priorities of standardized testing, unique educational plans, discipline, school counseling, and occupational, speech, and physical therapy. The question becomes how much a school can cram into a day and where the responsibility of the school stops and the parent starts, and vice versa.

Responsibility Has Changed in Education

We often make the mistake of simplifying children as just little adults. Hence, when they do and say something, we place their words on equal footing with what their teachers or principals tell us about them. Children are not little adults because they are still socially, emotionally, and physically developing to one day (hopefully) be those wise adults we hope for them to evolve. Children, in reality, have very little control or inherent responsibility in the world. They do not choose their school, teacher, the school day hours, or most aspects of their lives. Concurrently, if the child is afraid of punishment or the pain of disappointing adults, they are more apt to be untruthful. Many experts argue that being dishonest (to some extent) is a typical developmental stage of growth.[2] By age four, 90 percent of children understand how to lie, and they only become better at it and more subtle at this skill over time.[3,4]

Additionally, have you ever seen your child do something that seems so out of character, dangerous, impulsive, or absent-minded and asked yourself, "What were they thinking?" The answer is that our children are often incapable of thinking as we do. In a child, the brain's prefrontal cortex, which controls planning, reasoning, judgment, and impulse, is not fully developed until they are twenty-five.[5] This means that the ability of your child to function and make the same rational and well-planned decisions and thoughts is not the same as that of adults. They are akin to drivers who can put their foot on the gas pedal but have faulty brakes. Inevitably, they will run into things, have accidents, and make errors.

Does this imply that we should not believe in our children? No, of course not. It means that when we take their word over their teacher (or school administrators) repeatedly, we model for them that they do not have to be responsible for their actions. It also states that they are on the same social level as adults, which creates a structural imbalance. Further, it blurs the very boundaries between adult and child as well as teacher and student.

Are there times when a teacher picks on a student or when the teacher, administrator, or educational system is blatantly in the wrong ... absolutely! However, we must respect that the balance of our child's behavior, attitude, and work habits must ultimately be the child's responsibility. The teacher's role is to ensure that your child takes ownership of these areas. When we interfere with this by not working with the teacher, we create what is known, from counseling theories, as triangulation. Triangulation is a dysfunctional relationship pattern when two parties (teacher and student) are involved in a form of conflicted communication (the grades or behavior of the child being responsible) and involve a third party (the parent) to distract from the issue between the other two. The problem becomes it deflects from the child's responsibility as the teacher and parents discuss who is responsible for the student's role without the most critical party present ... the student![6]

What Is Our Goal in Education?

When a child enters the doors of a school, the goal should be to educate them for a future that current educators only have a fleeting sight of ever glimpsing. This means a well-balanced child can work academically, emotionally, and socially in society. A child who can assert their needs and still work within a team is required. This requires a balance of students who can assert themselves without resorting to aggression or being so meek that they cannot be influential members of the workforce or society.

Table 6.1 gives an idea of the middle spectrum that we seek for our children in their journey through the educational system.

Whose Job Is It Anyway? Yours, Mine, and Theirs . . .

Education relationships are a triad of responsibilities that must be shared among teachers, parents, and students. As in any organization, each has a succinct role in the organization's work. When one party significantly overlaps with the job of the other, accountability becomes blurred, and the educational institution's mission can become less effective or break down completely. Although sometimes, one party must briefly infringe on

Table 6.1 Looking at the Spectrum of Assertiveness and Conflict Resolution

Overly-Passive Student	Well-Adjusted Student	Overly Aggressive Student
Tends to turn anger inward	Express anger in an assertive fashion	Tends to turn anger toward others
May have trouble making friends	Has little trouble making friends	Has trouble keeping friends
Tend to feel more helpless	Feel helpful	Feel hopeless
Has anxiety about joining activities	No issues with joining activities	Has trouble staying in activities

[1] Novick, B. J. (2019). *The angry child: What parents, schools, and Society Can do*. Rowman & Littlefield.

A Responsible School

another's role, it cannot be for an extended period or become habitual as this leads to challenges with the hierarchy and clarity of the job of each party.

Textbox 6.1 shows who should typically be responsible for which role.

Textbox 6.1: The Ideal Designated Role of Each Stakeholder

Teacher/Educator's Role

- Provide a curriculum of the highest quality possible for the students.
- Work with students at varying levels to reach the standards for each grade based on state and national requirements.
- Offer reports on student progress regularly and consistently.
- Explain to parents and develop resources to help students reach optimal levels of academic proficiency.
- Ensure that they are up to date on professional development so that they can educate using methods that are the most up to date for all student abilities.
- Provide constructive feedback to parents and students to help them grow optimally in their academic success.
- Work and provide support to students regardless of academic level and ability.
- Be respectful and professional to parents and students and expect them to be the same.

Parent/Guardian Role

- Parents should be certain their children get to school and that someone is available when they get home regularly and in a timely fashion.
- Help their children complete homework and work assigned at home without doing the work for them.
- Support and encouragement for their children on the importance of academics and celebrating successes.

- Meet with teachers at conference times, sign the necessary paperwork, and review school websites to stay informed about what is happening within the school.
- Model and enforce appropriate behavior.
- Provide proper mental, emotional, physical, social, and financial support to their child.
- Support school rules and laws regarding their children.
- Keeping educators apprised of any situation at home that may affect their children at school.
- Return calls and inquiries from school personnel in a timely fashion.
- To be supportive of their child's education of their child as a whole.

Student Role

- Get to class promptly and be prepared with all necessary materials.
- Finish all assignments by the time they are required to be completed.
- Do homework and study regularly in preparation for tests and assignments.
- Follow all school rules and policies in a respectful manner.
- Take care of personal and school property.
- Request help when needed from teachers.
- Make positive choices and accept the consequences for their actions.
- Demonstrate respect and tolerance for those who have differing views, beliefs, or are otherwise dissimilar from you.

Suspension Is Not the Answer to Encouraging Responsibility

Earlier, we discussed the child with the "all-inclusive vacation." This child has a bedroom with all the necessary technology, sleep, food, and material items. They have little to no encouragement to do anything outside this bedroom because it contains all they want; they never feel the need or motivation to leave their room. School represents a distraction from this because the child will be forced to do things, such as schoolwork, that they would prefer not to do.

What would be the worst consequence a school could provide to students who do not take responsibility and love to be in the all-inclusive vacation room? How about a suspension? Is it a school sanctioned ability to stay in that room all day or all week? The problem with out-of-school suspensions is that they are simply ineffective. Research by the American Institutes of Research details that out-of-school suspensions are ineffective in changing behavior. Additionally, the harsher the suspension, the more it is correlated with a negative impact on the pupil's future academic performance, behavior, and attendance.[7]

If Not Suspension . . . Then What?

Every aspect of an educational system should provide an opportunity to learn. Disciplinary sanctions are also essential to understanding what society has in store for the child when they make positive and negative decisions. When we speak of waiting until a child gets into the "real world," public education is that incubator to prepare the child to get out of the nest and spread their proverbial wings in that real world. School is not an actual society in itself, but it should be an accurate facsimile of the world to learn what is necessary for success within it.

How do we do this? The push for disciplinary sanctions is called restorative discipline. The premise of this concept is: how do we make amends for the mistakes we made to our school community/society at large? The punishment fits the crime, so to speak, in that, a detention or suspension is not always the answer to teach children how to solve problems that do not function in society.

What Exactly Is Restorative Discipline?

School discipline often seems out of sync with the nature of the infraction. For instance, if you bully a peer and are given a detention or suspension, it is certainly a consequence. However, what does it do to develop the educational community, improve the school climate, or help the student accept responsibility and restore the relationship with the victim? The answer is, well, generally, not much.

Restorative discipline puts the onus back on the student. It requires the pupil to consider who was impacted by their actions, how they were impacted, and what the student can do to repair the issue and make reprimands.[8] Restorative discipline looks to be a proactive intervention, asking what can be done to intervene, how to better the school community interactions, how educators can improve, reduce, or prevent the behaviors again, and how to develop a conflict resolution solution to hold all parties accountable.[9]

The Easy Restorative Discipline Real-World Classroom Rules

Some of the restorative discipline interventions can be so common sense that they may seem minimal or obvious; however, here are a few to consider:

- When you hurt someone's feelings . . . apologies must be sincere: Apologies must include a plan for correcting your wrongdoing. Knee-jerk reactions of empty apologies with no plan for making reprimands for repairing the student they have harmed are not accepted.
- The student is responsible for keeping their word: Students are responsible for doing what they say they would do or explaining why they could not do so directly to the person they disappointed. Further, if you do not complete your obligations (such as your schoolwork or homework), you will have to complete them at some time that is not to your liking or choosing.
- If you break it: When you irresponsibly break a relationship or property, it is your job to try to repair it (this applies to both property and classroom/peer relationships).
- If you are upset, you must say what you need: Tantruming or sulking is one of the least effective ways of demonstrating anger or sadness. Instead, the student who is angry or sad must also provide some ideas of what may work to remedy the issue.

The Magic of "I" Messages Again

Perhaps one of the areas that students must be most responsible for is how they handle conflict. Conflict will inevitably arise in society, the workplace, school, and the home. According to the job-hiring website Indeed, the top six skills an employer is looking for are communication, leadership, teamwork, adaptability, interpersonal, and self-management skills.[10] If we prepare students to be responsible employees, we must help them understand how to work with various persons with varying views and motives.

The "I" Message is not a new concept; the American psychologist Thomas Gordon, PhD, coined it in the 1960s when teaching parenting enrichment programs.[11] Half a century later, psychologist and marital expert Dr. John Gottman found that the "I" Message was compelling in its application to marital and family discord.[12] The beauty of the "I" Message is that although it creates profound changes in how responsibility is taken in conflict, it is straightforward to apply.

Below is the format for an "I" Message:

- I feel _____ (How you feel)
- Because _____ (Why do you feel that way?)
- So I _____ (What supports your opinion and what do you need?)

"I" messages for students are very effective because they state precisely what the student is feeling. This avoids others having to mind read the emotional barometer for the other person and thus avoids assumptions. It also forces students to take responsibility for understanding and expressing their feelings rather than spouting profanity or name-calling.

Secondly, when students have to explain why they feel the way they do, they have to give a reason for what caused their current emotional state. In doing so, their peers have a strong understanding of what they are feeling, and it avoids tantrums and pouting, which allows students to defer their ownership of the origin of the conflict.

Finally, once you tell another what you need, you are contributing to part of the solution versus just pushing the solution for the conflict onto someone else. This teaches students an important lesson in responsibility; it is not just about a single party having to solve the problem but the creation of potential solutions for both parties to ponder.[13] Such a skill is an important life lesson in that your boss at work will not just expect you to come to them with problems but also potential solutions.

Restorative Discipline . . . the Details

In a world where public education focuses primarily on curriculum, programming, and standardized testing, it is essential to know that restorative discipline does not fall into any of these domains. According to Costello and Wachtel, the overall objective of restorative discipline and practices is to create students who are happier, more cooperative, more productive, and more likely to make positive changes. Further, it changes the role of those in positions of authority to work collaboratively with students rather than perceived as doing things to or for them.[14]

Some restorative discipline and practice interventions in schools are a subtle shift from how conflict, disagreement, and discipline may have been handled previously in education. For instance, those using this mindset will avoid criticizing the student and instead focus on the perception of what the student might hear. These statements are similar to "I" statements and aim to let the person speaking to know precisely how their behavior is impacting the other student or faculty member hearing it. They focus on the behavior and not the character of the students themselves.

For instance, affective statements may look like what is given in Table 6.2.[15]

Restorative discipline practices also look very different in terms of consequences within the educational institution. In the past, the focus was on punishing the offender for an action in school that would violate a rule or policy. Let us take the issue of bullying; for instance, a principal would suspend the bully, which would generally be the end of that interaction. Discipline from this punitive framework punished the perpetrator but never gave the victim a voice, and thus they may have never learned how to assert themselves (allowing for the potential of repeated victimization). Additionally, it rarely teaches the bully how to empathize with the target, reflect on their actions, or offer any form of redemption directly to the target.

Table 6.2 Using Affective Statements in the Classroom

Typical Classroom Statement	What the Student Hears	Better Affective Statement
When you talk when I am talking you are being rude!	The student is accused of being a rude person and ignores the reason why the student wants to be heard.	When I hear you talking at the same time I am, I feel discouraged because I would also like others to hear me. Would you please consider raising your hand when you want to speak?
I don't want to see you bullying Sarah	The teacher made a judgment call without knowing all the facts of the matter.	When I saw you pushing Sarah, I was very scared since I want everyone in our school to be safe. Would you be able to tell me what is happening between both of you?
Don't do that . . .	It does not tell the student what to do, and there is a sense of blame and accusation.	When I heard you say that, I was disappointed because I value everyone's respect in our school. Could you tell me what you were thinking that made you say that?

Let's say, for instance, the theoretical bully has to write a letter of apology to the targeted student, do a project about bullying, or read a book about someone bullied. They understand and become responsible for their behavior versus simply enduring punishment and not learning other means of handling the issue. It requires three essential aspects for improvement: reflecting on what they did wrong, attempting to repair the ruptured relationship, and learning a better way to address this behavior in the future. This triad of interventions creates a more balanced relationally-based dynamic for discipline.[16]

Disciplinary sanctions of the past were often reactive rather than proactive. We punished a student for their actions with no preparation for future knowledge of how to adapt their choices more effectively. Restorative discipline forces the students to identify why they did what they did. It teaches students that learning the reason for their behavior is part of their education by recognizing their own self-awareness and understanding. This lesson of self-awareness can take a lifetime to master, yet it is never too early to begin the steps of learning the nature of oneself.

When we punish students, everyone focuses on what we will do *to* them; parents ask that question, students worry about it, and the administration enforces it. Yet, this mindset never asks *how* we will repair what was done. If

I put graffiti all over the boy's bathroom and you suspend me, that is great, but you still have permanent marker all over the bathroom stalls. A better question is, how will *I* repair, be responsible for *my* actions, and make *my* educational community whole again?

Restorative justice seeks to highlight the necessity of trust and inclusion school-wide. It requires the collaboration of all parties in the conflict. Doing so bolsters trust, understanding, and a more inclusive classroom environment. Building peer mediation, in which a student answers to his peers and educational society educators for their actions, emulates a model of society in which you are ultimately responsible for answering your actions to your peers. Further, it seeks to teach all students that they are a community and are accountable for monitoring and improving their school climate systemically.[17]

Kids Cannot Learn Conflict Resolution without Having Conflict

Learning how to address conflict can be a very challenging exercise for students and, indeed, for anyone. We can easily slip into fight or flight mode when engaged in altercations. During this time, our blood and energy are focused on our extremities and away from our brain. The hormones cortisol and adrenaline course through our body and create a tunnel vision in which it can be challenging to think through rational problem-solving and thought. We are primed to run or enter a physical conflict. As blood goes away from our brains, we react angrily if someone asks, "What are you thinking?" The answer is we generally are not.

We may blame, yell, and scream during this, but taking responsibility for our emotions and actions is difficult. Legendary psychologist Dr. John Gottman refers to this as flooding.[18] Like a vehicle engine with too much fuel to operate, our brains do the same thing. Often, we make terrible decisions when we are angered, impulsive, and sometimes even dangerous. Of course, children are no different and are even worse in this domain due to a lack of how to develop patience when confronted with solid conflict.

Having children discuss conflict resolution in real time can help them practice this skill. Restorative circles allow children to sit in a circle and discuss issues with peers they are in conflict with and develop constructive conflict solutions. An adult's role is to create a supportive and safe place where they can bring up concerns, and the adult can coach and guide how to discuss conflict or sensitive topics with more planning and forethought. The essential aspect is that the faculty can provide practical and real-time feedback on taking responsibility for one's actions, foster better practice in conflict resolution, and enhance the school community.[19]

You Need Consistency to Learn Responsibility

In society, we need some form of consistency to know how we are supposed to function and what is expected of us from the larger community. For instance, due to your respective state's law, you could, or should, know the rules and penalties for speeding. Therefore, you are clear about the law and the risks you will face when you break such societal laws. Laws should be consistent and predictable across the board within your region. If you went to another country, rules and laws could be radically different. For instance, simply chewing gum in Singapore can result in a fine or even jail time.[20]

Are our schools like this? Do students fully comprehend what the rules and consequences are? Can they tell their parents and teachers, if asked, what the rules and consequences are in school? Do administrators all provide these disciplinary consequences equitably and with equal accountability? Does a student have the same result for a relatively minor infraction (like using their cell phone) from classroom to classroom? If not, are these consequences left to the energy and emotion of the teacher and thus inconsistently doled out with reckless abandon? Such implementation of the school rules can lead to an unpredictability of responsibility and an extreme lack of consistency in the overall school climate for which all members are accountable.

Without Appropriate Placement of Student Responsibility, Teacher Burnout Will Continue

One of the primary reasons for educator burnout is the judgmental nature of parents who are constantly critical of teachers and/or are not supportive of their child's education as a primary goal. Concurrently, if parents do not respect the educator's boundaries or professional opinion, this can ultimately promote a high degree of educator burnout.[21]

In the past, many thought the pressure of perfectionism that teachers would place upon themselves set the stage for burnout (as in many other professions). Yet, a study in the Journal of Anxiety, Stress, and Coping, surveyed 118 educators teaching an average of two decades contrasts with that train of thought. Generally, vocational burnout stems from sensitivity to criticism or a desire to do one's role with the self-inflicted (or peer-inflicted) impossibility of perfection. In this study, however, the desire for perfection came from parents versus colleagues, administrators, or students. Though this is just one study, statistics of one-third of teachers leaving the profession within three years and almost 50 percent in five years bolsters these survey results. According to a 2022 Gallup Poll, the burnout rate for educators in K-12 is 44 percent, making it one of the highest rates of any industry. Concurrently, most educators would not recommend college students to enter the field of education.[22]

Educators and parents are all working toward the same goal: student progress and working toward taking responsibility for their success. Somehow, this can become distorted in the name of parents standing up for their child due their belief of their son/daughter being picked on or the belief that the teacher is unfair toward their child by overly pointing out academic or behavioral issues. Political concerns over the curriculum being taught and the role of public education are also thrown into the mix in which non educators decide the future of education and are critical of those teaching. Ultimately, schools work only when parents and educators provide a unified front toward a child's success versus when they work against each other as antagonists.

Schoolwork, homework, and behavioral expectations are the "on-the-job training" of children. When parents make excuses or shield their children from these roles, they teach children they are not responsible for their role as students. Further, this implies that the teacher's job is both in the teaching *and* learning aspects of the youth's education. The boundaries are for teachers to teach and students to learn.

Preparation for Anger, Frustration, and Stress

In public education, physical education is taught as a standard curriculum in schools nationwide. Almost every school has a gymnasium for youth to work out their bodies and enrich their physical health. However, how many of our schools have a designated place for a child to work out their emotional health? It would seem the majority of our schools simply do not have such a designated controlled environment for youth to manage and take responsibility for their emotional health. This is despite the growing needs of an increasingly stressed. The anxiety-ridden student body has grown by 40 percent since the decade previous to the Covid-19 pandemic.[23]

Escaping from Class . . . But to What?

The question becomes, when our children elope from a classroom to get away from the anxiety or stressors of class, where exactly can they go? Some may say the school counselor's office, but what if the counselor is seeing someone or if counselors do not have an independent place they can go to? When we think of an office, it is more akin to a classroom setting than a place for the sole purpose of de-escalation. Enter the reset room, also known as a Zen Den, whose sole purpose is to provide a space to decompress and relax. It is differentiated from a "time out" room in which students, in the latter case, are brought to a relatively bare room to de-escalate tantrums or out-of-control behaviors by having little to no stimulation in their environment. The reset room should be looked at as a place of calm and serenity, not a place of seclusion. Should a school not have a specific room, a part of a room can be devoted solely to a reset room. Setting aside such a space in an office or empty classroom is permissible, provided such a room is limited in noise and stimulation.

For an elementary/middle school reset room (see Table 6.3) for a suggested inventory of what should be included.[24]

It is important to note that a "reset room" still requires faculty to supervise the student. However, it allows a student to begin the process of self-soothing from frustration and anger, which is a needed life skill.

Frustration and Learned Helplessness

How often have educators heard from students that they "can't do something?" When children begin a pattern of giving up prematurely, they start walking

Table 6.3 Suggested Inventory for a Reset Room

Elementary/Middle School Reset Room Suggested Inventory
Crayons, markers, paper, and/or clay to allow students to express their emotions in a manner aside from verbally.
A way of playing calming music, environmental sounds, or a white noise machine.
Lights that are dim and are not fluorescent.
Seating that is comfortable such as pillows, bean bags, or reclining chairs.
Manipulatives that allow a student to distract focus away from anxiety, stress, or anger.
Carpet that a child can lie down on comfortably.
A weighted blanket (optional)
A place that is far away from place where children are routinely disciplined within the school (if possible)

down a road of learned helplessness in the classroom. Why? Because the general response that the youth may hope to receive is a constant stream of confirmation from adults that "they can do it." or "I believe in you." Both statements, on the surface, present as innocuous and well-intentioned responses. While this may be true, the answer to the student's frustration lies perpetually outside their locus of control. That is because some pupils always look outside themselves for validation and support and toward a figure of authority.

As students continue their academic careers, they may look toward something or someone outside of themselves for validation that they are capable or successful in other aspects of their lives. This leaves educators wondering what an appropriate response would be toward a student who exclaims, "I can't do it." The answer stems from encouraging the student to find encouragement and support in the most essential and eternal element of their mental health and control: themselves.

For instance, the teacher can encourage the child to debate their distorted thinking process by asking, "Tell me three things you did successfully today?" "What are three things you did right and are proud of about school today?" Students must be taught that just because they have a disheartening or damaging thought does not automatically make it so. Children should be taught to be responsible for debating their thought processes, questioning their distorted thinking patterns, learning from them, and self-soothing when things are not going the way they initially planned.

Part of the challenge for students is that when they think something in their heads, they consider it 100 percent true without question.[25] Developmentally younger students (K-2) often express what is known as fantasy thinking, in which they assume that whatever happens in their world is caused by what they think.[26] This can be characterized in the age-old childhood rhyme of "Step on a crack, and you'll break your mother's back." Such a rhyme is a prime example of a younger child's cause-and-effect thinking process. Thought processes are not that simple, and students have to begin to question the validity of their thoughts with logic and evidenced-based thinking versus from a fantasy or solely emotional perspective.

How Do We Get Parents More Involved and Take Responsibility in Our Schools?

Since the Covid-19 pandemic, over 80 percent of educators have noted an uptick in behaviors within the United States public school systems.[27] This has created a lot of finger pointing as to if this is the result of over permissive parents, increased bullying in schools, or an overwhelmed and overburdened educational system? The answer lies likely in a combination of all of these elements and is idiosyncratic to each school and region.

One of the suggestions is to have schools play a more active role in parental as well as student education. That is, having schools teach parenting enrichment programs to find effective ways of dealing with children's behavior within the home that will carry over (theoretically) into the school and community settings. Though this seems like a well-intentioned plan, it has one obstacle that stands it its way; getting the parents most in need of these programs to attend. The refrain from many educators is that they get the parents of the students who are most accountable for their child's behavior and not the "at-risk" students and parents that they most want to target.

The following are some suggestions to get "at-risk" students' parents/guardians more involved in both parental and student enrichment programs:

1. Go Where the High-Risk Students Live: Find where the majority of your at-risk students live and hold the programs at those locations. Sometimes you can find a condo or apartment complex, clubhouse or community center to give you the space at no cost by

helping them see the benefit of improved parenting skills in their community.

2. Offer food/dinner. Food equals attendance. Dinner is one less meal that a parent has to prepare. This is especially important when families struggle to find money for food. Also, attendance tends to be better toward the end of a month when food stamps may be exhausted. Sometimes local restaurants may even consider donations in exchange for free advertising.

3. Have children and parents involved at the same time: When children are involved, parents are usually not far behind. If you can encourage the children to be excited about an activity then you just have to schedule your parenting enrichment program at the same time.

4. Choose topics that are long on practicality and short on theory. Parents who are struggling to keep their heads above water are most interested in what they can use right now. Keep topics current and create a curriculum that addresses the most practical topics. Break the topics down so they can be handled in one night (e.g., "How to Deal with Temper Tantrums" or "How to Get Your Child to Listen". Session titles that are too vague or too complex such as "Family Communication" will not generate as much interest.

5. Offer other resources as well. Most at-risk parents are dealing with difficult issues such as unemployment, illness, abuse, etc. If possible, ask local social services agencies to be present so they can answer questions and distribute appropriate materials.

6. Advertise everywhere. Sending a flyer home with a child usually won't cut it, so you need to work harder to get the word out. Find out where these parents look at fliers (community centers, grocery stores). The best thing to do is to make individual phone calls to the parents you want there. Does it take more time? Yes, but it is better than wasting your time conducting a program in a roomful of empty chairs. Also, be sure to encourage those who did attend to spread the word to other parents.

7. Make it fun. Think of activities that parents and children can do together. Make it memorable for both parties.

8. Involve the teachers. Ask teachers to give out extra homework passes to students whose parents attend. Encourage students by

having their teachers (who are usually the most familiar figures in a child's academic life) be present at the programs.

9. Give things away. Check your district's policy on giveaways first, but sometimes the PTA will help with door prizes or other freebies the parents and children can take home.

10. No RSVP (répondez s'il vous plaît). You probably won't get an accurate number anyway.

11. Keep it short. The actual parenting enrichment program should not be longer than an hour. Focus on quality versus quantity. But remember to add time for a question-and-answer period.

12. Call and say "thank you." Have a sign-in sheet so you can call to thank those parents who attended. This will also be your list to call when promoting the next program session.

13. Look for grants. You may be able to find private grants to fund some of your parenting programs. If your district has a designated grant writer, this person may be helpful.

14. Encourage; don't discourage. It goes without saying that parenting programs should be positive. Let parents know that you are trying to enrich the skills they have, not criticize or monitor what they already do. Many parents have had bad experiences with schools, child protective services or other agencies or institutions. Don't turn them off by complaining about the job they are doing.

15. Make social service agencies aware of your programs. If you are aware of private counselors or social service agencies that are working with your families, ask these individuals to encourage parents to participate in your programs.[28]

7 **Too Easily Deterred**
Resiliency, Self-Discipline, and Children

Marshmallows and Responsibility... Not Just Fluff

In the 1970s, psychologist Walter Mischel, PhD at Stanford University, conducted experiments on how young children take responsibility.[1] The study's concept was straightforward: a child could choose between taking a single marshmallow now or receiving two marshmallows if they waited until the researcher returned. The researcher would then leave the room for fifteen minutes, and when they came back, the child would be given two marshmallows if they did not eat the first one as a reward for their patience.

The study did not end here, however, as these youths were tracked into adulthood, and it was determined that those who were able to respond with self-discipline and delay gratification for the two marshmallows had better SAT (Scholastic Aptitude Test) scores and educational success as adults, were in better physical shape, had lower body mass indexes, and had more success than the latter. The study taught an important lesson: the younger a child can establish responsibility and self-discipline, the better the likelihood they develop into competent, accountable adults.[2]

How Can Marshmallows Determine Responsibility and Success?

Of all the skills that we hope children will learn, what are the most essential? Perhaps none are more important than perseverance, resilience, and patience. The unfortunate matter for many of our children is that they will meet with failure at one point or another. Doors will close, they will not get that dream job on the first try, and office politics will not get them the job they are qualified for because someone knows someone. They can become jaded, blame others, and shift the focus of control from their responsibilities to those of someone else and become apathetic.

Yet, isn't any worthwhile skill or job correlated with the amount of time, self-discipline, and patience?[3] Our upcoming generations are having their concentration evaporated by voluntarily subjecting themselves to only quick soundbites of technology that only encourage very short periods of focus before they swipe away in favor of the next video blurb or experience. A 2023-year review supporting this hypothesis reviewed the past twenty-three years of neuroimages of children and found that prolonged screen exposure changes the prefrontal cortex, which is responsible for adapting to new situations and working memory. Additionally, that same study indicated that children's brain cortexes have shrunk over the years, thus impacting reasoning and critical thinking. If you don't believe technology affects brain development, how many of us can still name the top ten phone numbers of our family and friends by heart or figure out how to get somewhere without GPS? Two decades ago it would have been expected skills to memorize important phone numbers and be able to read a map.

Therefore, the question becomes how we build resilience, discipline, and accountability traits for our children to succeed in school and eventually society. The key is to teach our children to be responsible for their own self-discipline. Like any other skill, this trait starts with being able to hold attention for a few minutes and gradually build that skill over time. Learning self-discipline requires deliberately setting aside some time each day for adults to teach mindfulness and the power of remaining present in the moment. Controlling one's impulses is a necessary life skill that will affect youth in every domain of their future lives.

In our society, we reward a result (i.e., the grade or the winning score) and miss the critical nature of giving one's best effort in the journey. As former tennis pro the late Arthur Ashe best stated, "Success is a journey, not a destination. The doing is more important than the outcome." In the intermediary struggle and being accountable for self-discipline, students develop patience and the ability to succeed in the most formidable of endeavors. Children should be celebrated for the youth's efforts rather than merely just to teach celebration of the end result. Success is a means of increasing a child's resilience and motivation to persevere in challenging circumstances.[4]

Children need to take responsibility and be resilient. They must be self-aware of their emotions and have a choice in responses. Ultimately, they should know that no one can "make you" do or feel something. Mindfulness allows youth to recognize that they can simultaneously have feelings or emotions and not react.

The 7 C's

In 2006, the American Academy of Pediatrics published a model of 7 C's for Resilience based on a previous model of only 5C's.

The 7 C's of Resilience which was derived from:

- **Competence:** Children can only become competent and confident by doing tasks and experiencing the frustration and patience gained through perseverance. Children cannot learn by having others do something for them or allowing them to give up prematurely.
- **Confidence:** Like competence, this trait can only come from children trying and doing activities independently. They must know their capabilities to build on the foundation of their competence and confidence in inherent abilities and skills. It cannot come from others doing things for children, or preventing them from attempting to learn new skills, due to fear of potentially failing. When adults do this for children, we subtly undermine their confidence that they can perform the respective activity adequately.
- **Connection:** Children cannot thrive in the world without some connection to others. From our birth, we seek and need connection for survival. This comes from a belief that someone (or many) believes in them and/or that they have a place to belong, such as clubs, sports teams, or civic organizations. It is important to note that the strength of these relationships is more important than the number of such connections. A child's view may sometimes be "more is better," however, they may not understand the concept of quality over quantity.
- **Character:** Values for children are shown by example rather than words. As mentioned earlier, children learn more by words versus actions; the same holds for character. Many schools employ character

education programs that include trustworthiness, citizenship, responsibility, fairness, caring, and respect.[5] It is important to note that a single curriculum or lesson does not teach character. Character is best taught when a child experiences a systemic view of these traits in their home and educational environment. It must be threaded into the curriculum, climate, and mission of both home, school, and extracurricular activities.

- **Contribution:** Children have little control over society, which is predominantly adult-run. They are told where they are going to school, who their teacher will be, what they will eat, and the situation they will live in, etc. This is why most young children are so eager to help their parents; it gives them some contribution to their family and the world. The contribution provides them with a sense of both purpose and worth. In social commentator and journalist Jennifer Warner's bestselling book When Achievement Culture Becomes Toxic-and What We Can Do About It, she defines this as *mattering*.[6] Wallace elaborates, "The idea of feeling valued by family, friends, and community for who you are deep at your core, and being relied on to add meaningful value to your family, schools, and communities. Mattering acts like a protective shield that buffers against stress, anxiety, and depression."

- **Coping:** Children will experience failure and stress no matter how much anyone attempts to shield them from these emotions and situations. Can they cope positively and productively or negatively, impulsively, and destructively? One way to look at this is how they handle the thoughts that come into their heads, whether resilient or rigid and destructive (see Table 7.1).

- **Control:** As mentioned earlier, most children's choices are controlled by adults. Gradually giving children more choices and responsibilities as they mature helps them assume control and responsibility. Conversely, giving them less responsibility and control leads to less maturity and acceptance of responsibility. When children have age-appropriate control, they build self-confidence; when they lack control, it fosters anxiety and helplessness. As a child grows, they outgrow their clothes, the television shows they are interested in and sometimes friendships. Likewise, they will outgrow the lessened expectations that are placed upon them and can be given ever more responsibility and choice as they mature.

Table 7.1 Productive Resilient Versus Destructive Coping Thoughts

Destructive Coping Thoughts	Productive Resilient Coping Thoughts
• Catastrophized Thinking: Always thinking about the worst-case scenario or that negative situations are actually much dire than they actually are.	• Questioning oneself if this situation is as bad as it seems? • Are my thoughts useful to solving the problem? • Testing thoughts to see if they are true instead of just believing them because you thought them.
• Mind-Reading: Assuming what another is thinking, feeling, or their motivations without any proof.	• Try to prove if your initial thought is correct or incorrect. • Look for evidence of your thought possibly being true or false. • What would you do if your thoughts were true? What would you do if your thoughts were false?
• Labeling: Placing labels on people, things, or thoughts. For instance using profanity, calling yourself or someone "a loser," or saying something "sucks."	• What are you specifically upset about? • When you call a peer a "jerk" what behavior are you upset about that you want changed (versus just name-calling)? • What specifically do you not like about a situation (versus a blanket statement like "this sucks.")? What strategies can you still try to do something that you may not feel capable of doing.
• Personalized Thinking: Everything that happens around you is because of something you did or did not do.	• When a child is young they tend to be egocentric and think the world revolves around them. As they grow older they should question their thinking. • Does this have anything to do with me or my behaviors? Or is it about someone else's responsibilities? • Most actions occur because others are thinking more about themselves than about you.
• Should, Must, Always, Thinking: Thoughts that everything has to be a certain concrete way for everything to work out or be successful.	• Ask what happens if you don't do what you think you should, must, or always do? • What other ways could a situation unfold that still may work out for you? • Does the child procrastinate for not feeling they could measure up to their expectations and so they refuse to even try?
• Big and Small Thinking: In this process a child will make the negative issues larger and, simultaneously, the positive attributes of a situation lesser. Therefore they will undermine their chances for accomplishments while inflating their belief in failure.	• Ask the child to remind themselves of their successes. • Ask another trusted adult to help remind the child if the negative consequences are really as scary as they think?

Ways of Thinking That Deteriorate Resilience

The following are modes of thinking that can decrease or deteriorate resilience in our children. It should be noted that all of us fall into these modes of thinking at one time or another. However, when these thinking processes become habitual, they can create difficulty with self-esteem, anxiety, or facing issues in a productive manner.

How Mindfulness Develops Resilience and Responsibility

At its best, mindfulness teaches that we *have* emotions; we are not *our* emotions. In other words, children have the responsibility and choice to experience emotions and not be controlled by or totally immersed in them. Being self-aware of emotions separate from oneself is vital to recognizing for children that they control their feelings, not vice versa. In other words, they alone are responsible for managing their emotional choices and handling the transient nature of their feelings. In doing so, it avoids shifting the blame to others who they falsely believe create and cause their emotional discord.

When emotionally reactive and angered, children become less able to solve problems. That reactive nature makes them think they must react based on these strong emotions. The most straightforward and effective answer (if they cannot remove themselves from the situation) is simply focusing on being calm and quiet and doing nothing to respond. It means focusing on the breathing, the calm, and the quiet by retreating inward.

Mindfulness can also mean that the child can use their untapped imagination. Doing so can look like taking an imaginary vacation to their favorite place and noticing sounds, smells, and visions to defer attention away from the stressful activity. Alternatively, just helping the child to be present in the moment by noticing their space, the smells, the sights, and the sounds of their current environment can serve to focus away from how they will respond and learn to self-soothe in the current moment. Sometimes the best answer to a response is simply no response at all.

Fear of Failure Does Not Build Resilience Either . . .

Failure is the way all of us learn the how to be successful and aware of our strengths and character. Unfortunately, when we keep children from the sting of failure, we also cripple their ability to be accountable, persistent, and resilient. To avoid failure, a child may take many steps to avoid anything that may lead to the remotest chance of not being successful. The concern is that one cannot learn the bounds of their strengths if they do not experience failures either. Additionally, fear of failure leads to anxiety and avoidance of anything that may resemble failure.

Sometimes, parents will try to defend their child for failing rather than figure out why they failed a test or some extracurricular activity. If children do not know the reason for their failure, however, they will repeat it continuously until they learn. If they never experience failure, they never learn the reason and develop the knowledge to succeed and blossom fully.

Failure teaches resilience strategies and alternative ways for success, but only if a child has the independence to make alternative decisions and figure out how to solve problems when an obstacle blocks their initial path to success. Not experiencing failure also does not teach how to believe you can be successful. Making excuses for failure, or blaming it on someone else, teaches the child that failure is not acceptable and responsibility for failure is never warranted.

Gratefulness Builds Resilience

It can be hard to be grateful in a world where social media highlights and encourages comparison of what one person has and another does not. Whoever has the latest smartphone or clothes can become the barometer for success or popularity. In a world like this, being able to treasure what you already have is often overlooked in favor of what you are getting next. The focus is always on getting more, having more, being more.

Journaling can help children be aware of what they have in a materialistic, future-focused world.[7] Often, journaling for younger generations can seem antiquated, and children may rebuff anything that requires manual writing as another academic task. Yet, there are many smartphone/tablet applications specific to journaling for gratitude.

For younger children, creating a gratitude jar in which children and parents write daily notes of what everyone is grateful for can achieve the same objective. Notes can be placed in the jar during dinner routines and/or holidays. When a challenging day or event comes up, your child can take a few notes out of the jar to remember what they are thankful for, thus bolstering their self-esteem and resilience.

Both activities can build a more gratitude-centered process in a world that highlights and encourages deficit thinking. Having children look toward who supports them, what tasks they have accomplished, and current and future-oriented opportunities can help them pull themselves out of a negative emotional tailspin. When we are in a negative emotional state, it is human nature to focus on the negative as confirmation and validation for why we feel the way we do and our irresponsible actions. Unfortunately, this behavior only creates a scenario where we ruminate longer or go into a deeper emotional hole, which can become a lifelong habit.

Fixing Our Minds toward a Growth Mindset

As discussed earlier, all children come with their idiosyncratic list of strengths and deficits. It should be noted, however, that research indicates that we all can improve and enrich our existing skills. We can build our muscles by lifting weights. We can bolster our brain capacities via knowing that working harder, gaining insight from trusted individuals, and learning can develop and enrich our talents and abilities. The ability to recognize this flexibility in capacity is known as a growth mindset.[8]

On the contrary, there is the fixed mindset that because one has only innate talents or skills, one can do nothing to change one's life. For instance, many schools have "gifted" children in their highest-level classes. Just from the verbiage, this implies that somehow they were blessed with some abilities that another child simply cannot reach unless they have "the gift."

The contrast of a growth mindset is that it teaches children to attempt a challenge and learn that all human beings never stop learning. These individuals see failure as an opportunity for learning and trying again versus a failure for which they cannot redeem themselves. Those with a fixed mindset shy away from challenges for fear of failure. A closed mindset also dooms one always to blame others for their lack of success or believe that their peers have some innate talent or abilities that they simply do not, or cannot, possess.[9] These children believe there is something inherently wrong with them that they have no accountability to change.

So, how do we develop a growth mindset? First, we should allow and encourage our children to know that we should expect imperfection as they attempt to navigate the world around them. That being said, we expect them to confront challenges head-on to the best of their ability. Additionally, they should not be afraid to receive critical feedback and learn from others. Finally, we expect them to be "the best me they can be." In other words, they are not to compare themselves to others (which leads to envy and unproductive jealousy). They are constantly expected to improve themselves to be their best version.

8 What Becomes of a Generation without the Ability for Responsibility or Accountability?

A Generation of Entitlement

What happens to a child who grows up in an environment where they are not subjected to understanding responsibility for their actions and their societal role in general? They run the genuine risk of feeling entitled when they enter the so-called real world. The difficulty is that they face an environment with little tolerance for those who don't earn their place through hard work, respect, and building a reputation.

This can impact several areas of the young adult's life because they do not understand the give-and-take characteristic of relationships. Such a philosophy on life produces the belief that they are the perpetual victim of others' ill will and that they deserve a lot more than the world gives them. After a period of frustration, they conclude that it must be the world that is out to get them, and they begin to look at other people as the cause instead of trying to change their behaviors for success. In time, they become bitter, self-centered, and insecure emotionally as they always look to others as accountable for their lack of success.[1]

Integrity Becomes an Endangered Trait as Well

Integrity is a crucial ingredient for responsibility and accountability. If you are not responsible, when no one is watching, as an adult you have an open invitation to do whatever you want to do with reckless abandon. When the authority figures are not the parents or the teachers, it becomes supervisors or law enforcement whom you run up against.

Such persons lacking integrity will rationalize their lies or actions as acceptable. Honesty is seen as a concept based on the shaky ground of a person's needs and wants. In relationships, they look toward how they will benefit rather than recognizing the interaction as a give-and-take in which each person attains something. In the workplace, such people will only see what is in it for them rather than being a team player, a quality valued in today's workforce. They may well climb the work ladder by stepping on the faces of those below them.

In relationships, they do not accept boundaries because they lack the empathy to juggle responsibility for their own feelings and others. They feel accountable only to their own needs or wants primarily and do not sense the necessity of being responsible to others. They are doomed to repeat their childhood history by not being able to admit they are wrong or display humility in their actions. Because of this blindness in self-awareness, they are doomed to make the same maladaptive decisions repeatedly.

Reactivity Versus Maturity

When you lack emotional maturity or the ability to be responsible for your actions, you likely have trouble managing your emotions as well. The ability to assertively communicate while keeping your emotions in check is a constant challenge. Hence, when you perceive someone is blaming you, instead of being introspective and seeing if you have any part in the responsibility, you go on the defensive and attack.

Emotional reactivity versus looking into oneself to what part you may have played in the conflict or situation is much easier. Like a child, the adult will kick, scream, yell, and curse versus trying to find out if the other person has some validity in what they are saying. Concurrently, they will overvalue and inflate their abilities and achievements to soothe themselves from the criticism of others. Never during these potential learning moments do they try to figure out how to better themselves and learn from the issue at hand and what they can improve upon. They will self-soothe with their own inflated b.s. of what they want to believe is true.

Emotional Immaturity Leads to an Emptiness

In childhood, we often learn the foundational skills for dealing with the world as adults. Some of the skills we know are helpful, yet other habits are not quite as productive for confronting the sometimes harsh world we emerge into as adults. As we get older, when under stress, we can very easily revert to some of our childhood strategies and attempt to adapt them for adulthood.

For example, when children get into trouble when they are young, they may try to distract from the conflict by saying something to their parents, such as "You hate me, I am so bad, no one likes me." When the youth uses these statements, it can cut to the very heart of the parent, who replies with comforting statements, such as "I love you, you are amazing, and everyone likes you." When this occurs, the situation is generally forgotten (with no potential consequence), and the parent has soothed the child's poor image of themselves and their guilt for perceiving that they were being so hard on their child for the time being.

This interaction seems harmless enough, except the child has focused on someone outside of themselves to validate them. If this occurs repeatedly, it can become an ingrained relational habit. As they age, they may extend these attributes to relationships with others by constantly looking at a boyfriend/girlfriend, friend, co-worker, or supervisor to fill the vacuum of their lack of belief in themselves. A positive comment by another important person in their lives validates them (at least for now). They have a perpetual hole within them that they must fill with someone else's approval. The accolades of others, however, are simply never enough because they cannot fill the void themselves by loving and believing in themselves. They are always hungry for more affirmations but can never feed themselves any when left to their own devices. It confirms the wise adage coined by author Alyssa B. Sheinmel, "You must love yourself before you can love anyone else."

When they enter relationships, they may quickly tire friends or significant others who recognize they cannot be responsible for another's emotional well-being. Their need for external validation becomes too much for anyone to handle. Further, when they feel that they are not receiving that validation, they become emotionally insecure and may overreact to believing that the person has stopped caring for them. This may lead to a pattern of lost relationships as they try to find those who can be accountable to fill their needs. The exhaustion others feel in meeting these expectations can be too much for many.

Self-Centered: It Is All about Me

Unsurprisingly, those who are not responsible for themselves feel they do not have to be accountable for others either. If you are not responsible for others, you risk being self-centered and only feeling answerable to your immediate needs and wants. This leads to finding egotistically what satisfies you at the time, regardless of what others may need from you as a spouse, parent, friend, or co-worker.

At times, these people seem very generous, which may catch those who relate to them off guard and make them think as thinking only about themselves. That being noted. However, they do this to inflate their egos and always attach strings to their gifts. They never do their favors or gifts without wanting something in return, now or in the future.

Mental Health Issues on the Rise

Earlier, we discussed how only 20 percent of those born between 1997 and 2012, compared to 39 percent of those born between 1946 and 1964, rated their mental health as "excellent" in a 2024 Gallup Poll.[2] According to the statistics by the National Alliance on Mental Health, some 50 million American adults have some degree of mental illness each year. With 19.1 percent of adults classified as having anxiety disorders, this represents the most significant percentage of mental health issues.[3]

Anxiety is often classified as a fear of the future or a perceived outcome that one cannot control. This is frequently caused by a shift to trying to be overly responsible for outcomes that are beyond one's control.[4] It is a tendency to blame oneself for situations or circumstances that one cannot control. In a sense, anxiety is due to trying to be responsible for areas in which one may not have accountability.[5]

A detrimental impact on one's self-esteem can come in the form of constantly comparing your life to an unrealistic yardstick of your family members, friends, or acquaintances. With the untamed wastelands that are social media, no one has to take responsibility for the accuracy of their statements, pictures, or comments to others, making these contrasts seem even more stark. When you are constantly connected to a trail of postings that falsely embellish another's perfect life, you believe you are inferior to others. Day after day, such exposure can lead to diminished self-confidence and depressive symptoms or anxiety. You have to keep up with another's false narratives.

Peer pressure, in both the child and adult realm, draws all back into the gravitational pull of social media for fear they are missing out on the posts of others. Worse yet, with cyberbullying, the subject of gossip might be the person who is not engaged in the current dialogue of social media conversation, which encourages constant monitoring of social media applications.

Lacking Corporate Responsibility

The children of today's society will be the executives of tomorrow's corporations. Many of the companies in which they will be employed have yet to be discovered using technologies that we can only glimpse in today's society. The question, however, is, what will the Amazons, Apples, and Googles of tomorrow look like regarding their accountability and responsibility to society? Corporate social responsibility is defined as a business that regulates itself toward society and promotes it as a primary objective, positively impacting its community.

Generating a pragmatic impact on society from the business paradigm requires that its executives consider demonstrating philanthropy, labor practices that are ethical and environmentally sound, and having their workers volunteer in causes that benefit society.[6] If our children of today are not geared toward responsibility to others, they are likely to gear their business practices aligned toward the goals of their self-interest and those of their investors. This will create a cycle of increased corporate greed and decreased obligation to the world around them.

AI and the Future of Responsibility

We are entering the first phases of artificial intelligence in our society. Artificial intelligence, or AI, is defined as the ability of computers to solve complex problems by being able to simulate human intelligence. In other words, machines are improving and learning, just like people. What does this mean for the future of responsibility and technology? As we become increasingly dependent on technology, it can lead to an ever more skewed perspective of what it means to be responsible.

How do we establish responsibility? At its basic level, we look at what someone says and does to determine that they are responsible for their words and actions. With AI, it is entirely possible to have video and audio that sounds and looks exactly like any person on the planet. This means that in the case of social media, for instance, people can create a simulated image of someone saying or doing something that is almost indistinguishable from the real thing. How will we know if it is the person responsible for their actions or someone behind the scenes creating a "deep fake" of that person? Who, and what, will we believe? What will this mean for cyberbullying, politics, and what we believe in the already confusing news cycle?

If we discuss responsibility in the future, we will also discuss the new term of responsible AI. What is responsible AI? This is an umbrella term for companies and social media creation of safeguards that assure artificial intelligence is transparent and organizations are accountable for their products. Responsible AI further means that these products are free from discrimination, secure, valid, and safe.[7] Without such assurances, the road ahead of corporate responsibility and trust becomes increasingly murky and uncertain.

Climate Change and Responsibility to the Environment

As the ocean waters warm, our globe is buffeted by more dangerous storms, tornadoes, and hurricanes. This will only become more of an issue as climatologists hypothesize that the average temperature will rise by approximately four degrees throughout the rest of the twenty-first century.[8] Rising sea levels and melting glaciers will further compound the problem and create a cycle of ever-greater natural disasters.

Addressing this issue is complex, requiring a societal and systemic approach to make a global impact in the future. Yet, the problem is so widespread that it can be difficult for the average individual to feel they can make a marked difference. From a more macro perspective, if one country does the responsible thing and makes a change to address this issue, it risks being left in the proverbial dust by others who produce materials unfettered by the chains of being responsible environmentally. Change must come in a form that all countries agree to operate under an umbrella that places climate above only profit.[9] As some countries are making significant profits with little regard for conservation, this can be a monumental task.

At the individual level, climate change requires sacrificing some aspect of what makes our modern lives convenient.[10] Do we cut down on transportation, electricity, or food consumption? If so, how much, and what level of inconvenience or cost, is needed before someone would want to refrain from doing so? Further, suppose it does not impact the current generation significantly. In that case, striving for accountability for something necessary to ensure a secure future for the generations that may come well after your own is challenging when you do not see the results firsthand. What about those political interests that would not only benefit but would be financially hurt by a change in climate change policy?

Education, Responsibility, and the Future

Education is a constantly evolving and fluid profession. It can often be cyclical in that the once-used curriculum is brought back, repackaged, and sold as a new and innovative idea. With the internet, we have seen technology evolve as never before. Students have become even more efficient in gathering information at the tip of their fingers in mere moments. Now, AI and virtual reality are in their pioneering stages as well. The question remains about what this next technology revolution will push education toward.

One avenue is the continued growth of online learning. This teaching method is expected to continue to grow at least 10 percent every year until approximately 2026.[11] This will require that responsibility in education to rest more and more with the student. Online learning often requires that students navigate independently through the curriculum without the teacher standing over their shoulder.

Additionally, online learning allows for more accessibility for those worldwide and creates less face-to-face and personalized education. Computer programs and applications that foster online education make fewer allowances for not meeting due dates or not following rigid expectations for each student that the educational platform follows. This means that students are more expected to be accountable for their actions and know what is expected of them rather than relying on educators. In many cases, they are also responsible for pacing themselves to complete necessary coursework or risk being left behind.

Public education may also focus more on utilizing social skills and emotional intelligence academically. The development of social-emotional learning curricula have been touted to help with socialization, and those schools that have a robust social-emotional learning program have seen student standardized scores rise an average of eleven points.[12] In a world that is becoming ever more standardized in testing, it would seem that academics and social skills should not be separate areas but integrated for maximum synergistic impact.

We have only just begun to scratch the surface of social-emotional learning and its integration into the conventional curriculum. Without the ability to combine Intelligence Quotient (IQ) and Emotional Quotient (EQ), an academically proficient student may flounder in the school of hard knocks, which is life. Technology is likely to help students tailor their emotional intelligence and social-emotional learning to the deficits and strengths of the individual pupil in the future as technology becomes more prevalent. Again, this will require the student to take responsibility for their future and work on their individual needs with less educator influence and more student control.[13]

The Future of Politics and Responsibility

Unfortunately, the country has been divided strongly along party lines. As a result, there is an inherent lack of trust among the opposing party regarding one's views and a belief that this party is not able, unwilling, or does not want to take responsibility for their actions or the country's fate. Finger-pointing and blame do not allow responsibility for either party or provide a blueprint for how the government should move forward. The Harvard Institute of Politics conducted a survey that reflects that those aged 18–29 find that 64 percent of those this age fear the future of America's democracy.[14] According to a 2023 Pew Survey, 72 percent of Americans believe the current governmental system is not working well.[15]

Answers to how the chasm of political divide will be solved in the future could be written in volumes and still not come to a satisfactory resolution for such a complex and difficult topic. A blueprint, however, exists from almost a century and a half ago. Abraham Lincoln could not have been in a more divisive political time for our country. A civil war plunged the country into the bloodiest time in our nation's history, and American citizens were literally divided into distinct countries.

One of the issues that made Abraham Lincoln among the greatest presidents and political leaders of all time was his ability not to try to boost himself by putting down the defeated South. He had no desire to punish his defeated enemies, nor to put them down, or those politicians who did not support his views. He took responsibility for his actions and behavior without finger-pointing or using his lofty position to further divide an already divided nation with rhetoric, hate, or one-sided political party gamesmanship. He had the rare ability to transcend politics and emotion to do what was best for the entire country. This is a difficulty, but necessary, stance to follow in terms of political responsibility in our current and likely future state.

Conclusion

Every generation points to the one that comes after it and utters disparagingly how easy they have it compared to their own rough-and-tumble upbringing. Whether it be how we drank out of water hoses and did not get sick, we rode bicycles without helmets, or we were allowed to roam the streets until the street lights came on, the familiar chant is that each generation has not been subjected to the turmoil of their previous ancestors. In years past there was even the belief that bullying was a rite of passage to toughen up somehow those who may be too weak to handle the school of hard knocks. Clearly, times and situations have changed and are continuing to do so.

It is very easy to speculate that the generational challenges in taking responsibility are a matter of simply needing to pull themselves up by the proverbial bootstraps and listen to the previous generations. They should listen and embrace the talk of how they trudged up the snow uphill both ways when they were their age. Unfortunately, the stories of life lessons have always fallen on deaf ears in each subsequent generation. History, as the story goes, is destined to repeat itself when we do not learn.

The more critical and accurate indication, however, is looking at the data of this generation when it comes to how they can handle the daily challenges that life indiscriminately throws at them. The CDC indicates that suicide is the second leading cause of death for ages 10–24 and is the origin of more deaths for this age group than almost all the illness that they could face combined.[1] The number of children that state they have chronic feelings of being sad or hopeless has surged by 40 percent between 2009 and 2019, which is one out of every three students. Further, a large survey by the CDC of 7,000 adolescents found that 40 percent found themselves feeling sad or hopeless.[2] Additionally, we see school shootings and violence that continue to make headline news on an almost weekly basis.

We can point to a multitude of prospective reasons for the decreasing mental health of the next generation. Some speculate it is an addiction to social media, cyberbullying, the erosion of families, substance abuse, etc. The post-traumatic stress of post-Covid-19, combined with a mental health system that is too overwhelmed, does not help the matter. Case in point, according to the Mental Health Association of New Jersey, the wait time for counseling in 2024 was a minimum of twelve to a maximum of twenty-two weeks.[3] Many rural areas around the country have few or no mental health professionals to care for children in crisis, not to mention parents who can pay the high costs of mental health services. As a result, children are waiting longer and longer and becoming ever more emotionally fragile.

Yet, when we completely shield our children from all consequences, we handicap their emotional growth. Childhood is a time to learn the necessary skills to one day be an adult. Education requires an understanding of the basic subjects, but it also requires testing on how to handle frustration and disappointment and believing in your self-worth and abilities. These tests have life lessons learned after the test, as the old adage goes. They are not the tests in which the school gives you the tests after the lesson. Unfortunately, our children can only pass these lessons by experience, responsibility, accountability and guidance.

No easier answers can be found because the answer lies in all of these variables and more. Responsibility is not something that any one person, organization, school, or generation can accept to make a change. This is not an answer. It needs to be a systemic and global effort for all to take accountability for what they can do for one child and one generation at a time.

In the end, each of us is responsible for our own lives, happiness, and futures. Our children may look to many places to find accountability or look towards distractions to avoid it. Time and time again they will learn the hard lesson of life that they are ultimately the responsible party. In the same notion, responsibility gives them a great power that they make the world theirs if they wield it appropriately.

Notes

Preface

1 State of the American teacher survey: 2024 technical documentation and survey results | Rand. (n.d.-b). https://www.rand.org/pubs/research_reports/RRA1108-11.html

2 American Psychological Association. (n.d.). *Studies show normal children Today report more anxiety than child psychiatric patients in the 1950's*. American Psychological Association. https://www.apa.org/news/press/releases/2000/12/anxiety

3 Ashton, Charlotte, & Turoman, Nora. (n.d.). *Too much information, too little time: How the brain separates important from unimportant things in our fast-paced media world*. Frontiers for Young Minds. https://kids.frontiersin.org/articles/10.3389/frym.2017.00023

Chapter 1

1 Lincoln and compensated emancipation in Kentucky. (n.d.-b). https://apps.legislature.ky.gov/LegislativeMoents/moments09RS/web/Lincoln%20moments%2020.pdf

2 Russell, P. (2017, September 13). *The 7 best leaders of the 21st century—and what you can learn from them*. HRZone. https://www.hrzone.com/lead/future/the-7-best-leaders-of-the-21st-century-and-what-you-can-learn-from-them

3 *Censorship in television*. (n.d.). Censorship and Government Regulation of Music RSS. https://wordpress.clarku.edu/musc210-cgr/rocking-the-media-censorship-of-rock-music-in-the-us/censorship-in-television/#:~:text=As%20a%20result%20of%20the,only%20from%20the%20waist%20up.

4. Fink, K. (2017, November 6). *12 things parents did in the '50s that millennial parents should bring back*. Romper. https://www.romper.com/p/12-things-parents-did-in-the-50s-that-millennial-parents-should-bring-back-3218481

5. C.Ht., Patricia Lantz (2023, May 3). *Key facts about family life in the 1960s*. LoveToKnow. https://www.lovetoknow.com/life/relationships/key-facts-about-family-life-1960s#:~:text=Growing%20Up%20in%20the%2060s,there%20were%20few%20helicopter%20parents.

6. Amy Morin, L. (2021, September 27). *How free-range parenting can benefit your child*. Verywell Family. https://www.verywellfamily.com/what-is-free-range-parenting-1095057

7. Los Angeles Times. (1994, November 13). The real '80s : If you think it was just a decade of greed, you missed the revolution. *Los Angeles Times*. https://www.latimes.com/archives/la-xpm-1994-11-13-tm-62250-story.html

8. Coleman, P. A. (2022, July 7). *A 1980s parenting style could save summer*. Fatherly. https://www.fatherly.com/parenting/1980s-parenting-self-reliant-kids#:~:text=Many%2080s%20parents%20practiced%20what,largely%20free%20from%20adult%20concerns.

9. *The anxious generation*. (n.d.). Jonathan Haidt. https://jonathanhaidt.com/anxious-generation/

10. Cunningham, J. (2020, June 12). *A triggered generation: Why 90s parenting failed and Central Park Karen is proof*. Medium. https://cunninghamjeff.medium.com/karens-meltdown-why-74d7591f7f86#:~:text=Haidt%20identified%20a%20problem%20known,result%20in%20outbursts%20like%20Cooper's

11. Greenthal, S. (2020, November 24). *How millennial parents are raising their children differently*. Verywell Family. https://www.verywellfamily.com/millennial-parents-raising-children-4158549#citation-5

12. McKenna, L. (2012, February 15). Explaining Annette Lareau, or, why parenting style ensures inequality. *The Atlantic*. https://www.theatlantic.com/health/archive/2012/02/explaining-annette-lareau-or-why-parenting-style-ensures-inequality/253156/

13. Miller, C. C. (2018, December 25). The relentlessness of modern parenting. *New York Times*. https://www.nytimes.com/2018/12/25/upshot/the-relentlessness-of-modern-parenting.html

14. Li, P. (2023, May 10). *Intensive parenting: Effects & 7 tips on how to quit*. Parenting For Brain. https://www.parentingforbrain.com/intensive-parenting/#:~:text=Intensive%20parenting%20is%20a%20parenting%20approach%20characterized%20by,to%20enhance%20their%20physical%2C%20cognitive%2C%20and%20social%20abilities.

15 WebMD. (n.d.). *Lawnmower parents: What are they?* https://www.webmd.com/parenting/what-are-lawnmower-parents

16 Mayer, B. A. (2023, November 16). *What is eggshell parenting and why you may want to avoid this parenting style.* Parents. https://www.parents.com/what-is-eggshell-parenting-7558796

17 Tsabary, S. (2010). *The conscious parent: Transforming ourselves, empowering our children.* https://openlibrary.org/books/OL30570895M/Conscious_Parent_The

18 Zapata, K. (2022, January 12). *All about conscious parenting and how to use it in everyday life.* Parents. https://www.parents.com/parenting/better-parenting/style/what-is-conscious-parenting-how-to-use-it/#:~:text=Conscious%20parenting%2C%20or%20CP%2C%20is,their%20child%20and%2For%20children.

19 Herndon, J. M. (2022, July 14). *Self-regulation definition and skills to practice.* Verywell Health. https://www.verywellhealth.com/self-regulation-5225245

20 Minkin, R. (2023, January 24). *Parenting in America today.* Pew Research Center's Social & Demographic Trends Project. https://www.pewresearch.org/social-trends/2023/01/24/parenting-in-america-today/

21 Centers for Disease Control and Prevention. (2023, March 8). *Anxiety and depression in children: Get the facts.* https://www.cdc.gov/childrensmentalhealth/features/anxiety-depression-children.html#:~:text=Facts%201%20Anxiety%20and%20depression%20affect%20many%20children1,in%202007%20and%20to%208.4%2520in%011%E2%012.%20

22 Osorio, A., Alker, J., Park, E., Burak, E. W., Lawson, N., & Dwyer, A. (2022a, December 9). *Research update: Children's anxiety and depression on the rise.* Center For Children and Families. https://ccf.georgetown.edu/2022/03/24/research-update-childrens-anxiety-and-depression-on-the-rise/

23 Miller, C. C. (2023, January 29). How parenting today is different, and harder. *New York Times.* https://www.nytimes.com/2023/01/29/upshot/parenting-survey-research.html#:~:text=And%20it%E2%80%99s%20not%20just%20how%20they%20feel%20E2%8094,survey%20of%203%2C757%20U.S.%20parents%20in%20that%20group

24 Sussex Publishers. (n.d.). *Parenting ain't easy.* Psychology Today. https://www.psychologytoday.com/us/blog/special-matters/201902/parenting-aint-easy

25 Osorio, A., Alker, J., Park, E., Burak, E. W., Lawson, N., & Dwyer, A. (2022, December 9). *Research update: Children's anxiety and depression on the rise.* Center For Children and Families. https://ccf.georgetown.edu/2022/03/24/research-update-childrens-anxiety-and-depression-on-the-rise/

26 Clifton, J. C., & Hrynowski, Z. (2024, April 23). *How happy is gen Z?* Gallup.com. https://news.gallup.com/poll/643721/how-happy-gen-z.aspx

27 University of Michigan Health System. (2016, April 18). *Most US adults say today's children have worse health than in past generations*. ScienceDaily.

28 https://www.nami.org/about-mental-illness/mental-health-by-the-numbers/

Chapter 2

1 McLeod, S. A. (2007). *The Milgram experiment*. Simply Psychology.

2 Badhwar, N. K. (2009). The Milgram experiments, learned helplessness, and character traits. *The Journal of Ethics, 13*, 257–89.

3 Fan, R., Zhao, J., Chen, Y., & Xu, K. (2014). Anger is more influential than joy: Sentiment correlation in Weibo. *PloS One, 9*(10), e110184.

4 Suler, J. (2004). The online disinhibition effect. *Cyberpsychology & behavior: the impact of the Internet, Multimedia and Virtual Reality on Behavior and Society, 7*(3), 321–6. https://doi.org/10.1089/1094931041291295

5 Slonje, R., Smith, P. K., & Frisén, A. (2012). Processes of cyberbullying, and feelings of remorse by bullies: A pilot study. *European Journal of Developmental Psychology, 9*, 244–59.

6 *The psychology of digital dehumanization*. (2023 August 9). Public Discourse. https://www.thepublicdiscourse.com/2023/08/89929/

7 *Armstrong's doping downfall*. (2023, February 16). Ethics Unwrapped. https://ethicsunwrapped.utexas.edu/video/armstrongs-doping-downfall

8 Thelukenorrisexperience. (2020, April 22). *How Charles Barkley's controversial "I am not a role model" Nike spot came to be*. Sportscasting. https://www.sportscasting.com/how-charles-barkleys-controversial-i-am-not-a-role-model-nike-spot-came-to-be/

9 Ngo, L., Kelly, M., Coutlee, C., et al. (2015). Two distinct moral mechanisms for ascribing and denying intentionality. *Scientific Reports 5*, 17390. https://doi.org/10.1038/srep17390

10 Blame culture is toxic. Here's how to stop it. (2022, February 11). *Harvard Business Review*. https://hbr.org/2022/02/blame-culture-is-toxic-heres-how-to-stop-it

11 Fast, N. J., & Tiedens, L. Z. (2010b). Blame contagion: The automatic transmission of self-serving attributions. *Journal of Experimental Social Psychology*, *46*(1), 97–106. https://doi.org/10.1016/j.jesp.2009.10.007

12 Parmelli, E., Magone, S., & Rosati, P. (2011). The importance of organizational change for improving healthcare performance. *International Journal for Quality in Healthcare*, *23*(3), 239–47.

13 *Understanding bots, botnets and trolls*. (n.d.). International Journalists' Network. https://ijnet.org/en/story/understanding-bots-botnets-and-trolls

14 Global prevalence and burden of depressive and anxiety disorders in 204 countries and territories in 2020 due to the COVID-19 pandemic. (2021, October 8). *The Lancet*. Retrieved January 24, 2023. https://pubmed.ncbi.nlm.nih.gov/34634250/

15 Bohn, R., & Short, J. (2012). Measuring consumer information. *International Journal of Communication*, *6*, 980–1000.

16 Centers for Disease Control and Prevention. (2023, October 16). *Data and statistics about ADHD*. https://www.cdc.gov/ncbddd/adhd/data.html

17 Psychology Education. (2023, August 6). *Lack of self-discipline: 13 root causes & 9 ways to fix it*. Believe In Mind. https://www.believeinmind.com/self-growth/lack-of-self-discipline/

18 Sinclair, A. (2024, February 14). *9 signs you were raised by well-intentioned but overbearing parents*. Global English Editing. https://geediting.com/signs-you-were-raised-by-well-intentioned-but-overbearing-parents/?utm_source=pocket_mylist

19 Sussex Publishers. (n.d.-b). *14 signs you were parentified as a child*. Psychology Today. https://www.psychologytoday.com/us/blog/healing-together/202001/14-signs-you-were-parentified-as-a-child

20 Rothman, A. M., & Steil, J. M. (2012). Adolescent attachment and entitlement in a world of wealth. *Journal of Infant, Child, and Adolescent Psychotherapy*, *11*(1), 53–65.

21 Chatrakul Na Ayudhya, U., & Smithson, J. (2016). Entitled or misunderstood? Towards the repositioning of the sense of entitlement concept in the generational difference debate†. *Community, Work & Family*, *19*(2), 213–26. https://doi.org/10.1080/13668803.2016.1134116

22 McKenna, L. (2012, February 15). Explaining Annette Lareau, or, why parenting style ensures inequality. *The Atlantic*. https://www.theatlantic.com/health/archive/2012/02/explaining-annette-lareau-or-why-parenting-style-ensures-inequality/253156/

Chapter 3

1. *2024 military strength ranking*. (n.d.). Global Firepower—World Military Strength. https://www.globalfirepower.com/countries-listing.php
2. *Program for international student assessment (PISA)*. (n.d.). National Center for Education Statistics (NCES) Home Page, a part of the U.S. Department of Education. https://nces.ed.gov/surveys/pisa/
3. *The benefits of debating*. (2021, February 10). The Edvocate. https://www.theedadvocate.org/the-benefits-of-debating/
4. Berner, Ashley. (2023, July 21). *What American schools can learn from other countries about civic disagreement*. The Conversation. https://theconversation.com/what-american-schools-can-learn-from-other-countries-about-civic-disagreement-169332
5. Morishita, Y. (2022, March 12). *Japanese work ethic—why Japan has such a great work ethic*. THE JAPANESE WAY. https://thejapaneseway.com/japanese-work-ethic/
6. Schwartz, Sherry. (2007, April). Educating the heart. *Education Leadership, 64*, 76–8.
7. Lewis, K. (2016, November 7). *How Japan prepares its children for Independence*. Savvy Tokyo. https://savvytokyo.com/japan-prepares-children-independence/
8. Pew Research Center. (2022, March 24). *1. The demographics of multigenerational households*. Pew Research Center's Social & Demographic Trends Project. https://www.pewresearch.org/social-trends/2022/03/24/the-demographics-of-multigenerational-households/
9. Brubaker, T. H. (1999). The four rs of intergenerational relationships: Implications for practice. *Michigan Family Review, 04*(1), 5. https://doi.org/10.3998/mfr.4919087.0004.102
10. Cockrell, M., Biggar, A., Gonzales, E., Stamp, T., & Jarrott, S. E. (2022, October 20). *The power of intergenerational connection*. ASA Generations. https://generations.asaging.org/power-intergenerational-connection
11. *Education rankings by country 2023*. (2023, April 13). Wisevoter. https://wisevoter.com/country-rankings/education-rankings-by-country/
12. *Happiest Countries in the World 2023*. (n.d.). https://worldpopulationreview.com/country-rankings/happiest-countries-in-the-world
13. Bildung. (n.d.) https://www.feelingeurope.eu/Pages/Bildung.html#:~:text=Bildung%20(%22education%2C%20formation%2C,both%20personal%20and%20cultural%20maturation.

14 Hamilton, David, & Gudmundsdottir, Sigrun. (1994). Didaktic and/or curriculum? *Curriculum Studies*, *2*(3), 345–50. https://doi.org/10.1080/0965975940020305

15 *Parental Pressure and Behavior May Put . . .* (n.d.). Caron Treatment Centers. https://www.caron.org/press-releases/parental-pressure-may-put-teens-at-risk-for-substance-use#:~:text=Nearly%20seven%20in%2010%20parents%20with%20a%20social,at%20times%2C%20social%20media%20makes%20parenting%20feel%20competitive

16 CBS Interactive. (2014, July 8). *Over-scheduling kids may be detrimental to their development*. CBS News. https://www.cbsnews.com/news/over-scheduling-kids-may-be-detrimental-to-their-development/

17 Sussex Publishers. (n.d.). *Parenting across cultures*. Psychology Today. https://www.psychologytoday.com/us/blog/parenting-neuroscience-perspective/202112/parenting-across-cultures

18 Glapa, A., Grzesiak, J., Laudanska-Krzeminska, I., et al. (2018). The impact of brain breaks classroom-based physical activities on attitudes toward physical activity in Polish school children in third to fifth grade. *International Journal of Environmental Research and Public Health*, *15*(2). https://doi.org/10.3390/ijerph15020368

19 Bernstein, R. (2022, April 29). *Child-rearing: Ms in marriage and family: Touro university*. Touro University WorldWide. https://www.tuw.edu/health/child-rearing-practices-different-cultures/

20 Stewart, S., Rao, N., Bond, M., McBride-Chang, C., Fielding, R., & Kennard, B. (1998). Chinese dimensions of parenting: Broadening western predictors and outcomes. *International Journal of Psychology*, *33*. https://doi.org/10.1080/002075998400231.

21 *The 7 distinct merits and extremes of Asian vs western parenting . . .* (n.d.). Says. https://says.com/my/imho/asian-parenting-vs-western-parenting

22 EmpathicParentingCounseling, & About The Author EmpathicParentingCounseling. Having extensively researched and studied the complexities of parenting. (2023, December 14). *Comparing Asian parenting vs western parenting: Understanding differences*. EmpathicParentingCounseling. https://empathicparentingcounseling.com/blog/asian-parenting-vs-western-parenting/

23 Ashley, M. M. (2023, August 17). *Gain face in China: Top 7 ways to boost your social standing*. MandarinMania.com. https://mandarinmania.com/gain-face-in-china/

25 Druckerman, P. (2014). *Bringing up bébé one American mother discovers the wisdom of French parenting*. Penguin.

26 Daniel, H. (2011, May 16). *Benefits of authoritarian parenting.* Benefits Of. https://benefitof.net/benefits-of-authoritarian-parenting/#:~:text=Benefits%20Of%20Authoritarian%20Parenting%201%201.%20Enhances%20safety,children.%20204%204.%20Creates%20responsible%20citizens%20

27 Caruso, M. (n.d.). *I'm an American parent in France. the French's parenting style is different, but it's made me secure in my own decisions.* Business Insider. https://www.businessinsider.com/french-vs-american-parenting-style-differences-2024-2

28 Caruso, M. (n.d.). *I'm an American parent in France. The French's parenting style is different, but it's made me secure in my own decisions.* Business Insider. https://www.businessinsider.com/french-vs-american-parenting-style-differences-2024-2

Chapter 4

1 WebMD. (n.d.-b). *Martyr complex: Causes, signs, and more.* https://www.webmd.com/mental-health/what-is-a-martyr-complex

2 McKay, M. (2016). *Self-esteem.* New Harbinger.

3 Redding, A., & Hill, N. E. (2021, April 28). The real reason young adults seem slow to "grow up." *The Atlantic.* https://www.theatlantic.com/family/archive/2021/04/real-reason-young-adults-seem-slow-grow/618733/

4 Responsible decision making: An introductory guide. (n.d.). *Positive Action.* https://www.positiveaction.net/blog/responsible-decision-making

5 Brandenburg, D. (2021, October). Consequentialism and the responsibility of children: A forward-looking distinction between the responsibility of children and adults. *The Monist,* 104(4), 471–83. https://doi.org/10.1093/monist/onab013

Chapter 5

1 *Sharing too soon? children and social media apps.* (n.d.). National Poll on Children's Health. https://mottpoll.org/reports/sharing-too-soon-children-and-social-media-apps

2 Muntingh, L. (2023, February 20). *18 internet safety statistics for 2022.* Screen and Reveal. https://screenandreveal.com/internet-safety-statistics/

3 Children's Online User Ages Quantitative Research Study. (n.d.-a). https://www.ofcom.org.uk/__data/assets/pdf_file/0015/245004/children-user-ages-chart-pack.pdf

4   Gallup. (2023, March 5). *How does the Gallup panel work?* Gallup.com. https://www.gallup.com/174158/gallup-panel-methodology.aspx

5   *What does children should be seen and not heard mean?* (2017, March 28). Writing Explained. https://writingexplained.org/idiom-dictionary/children-should-be-seen-and-not-heard

6   Coppola, G., Musso, P., Buonanno, C., Semeraro, C., Iacobellis, B., Cassibba, R., Levantini, V., Masi, G., Thomaes, S., & Muratori, P. (2020, July 30). The Apple of daddy's eye: Parental overvaluation links the narcissistic traits of father and child. *International Journal of Environmental Research and Public Health, 17*(15), 5515. https://doi.org/10.3390/ijerph17155515. PMID: 32751639; PMCID: PMC7432641.

7   Jabeen, F., Gerritsen, C., & Treur, J. (2021, March 2). Healing the next generation: An adaptive agent model for the effects of parental narcissism. *Brain Informatics, 8*(1), 4. https://doi.org/10.1186/s40708-020-00115-z. PMID: 33655460; PMCID: PMC7925789.

8   Sussex Publishers. (n.d.). *Introversion*. Psychology Today. https://www.psychologytoday.com/us/basics/introversion

9   *12 benefits of being an introvert*. A Great Mood. (2021, October 5). https://agreatmood.com/benefits-of-being-an-introvert/

10 Brummelman, E., Nelemans, S. A., Thomaes, S., & Orobio de Castro, B. (2017). When parents' praise inflates, children's self-esteem deflates. *Child Development, 88*(6), 1799–809. https://doi.org/10.1111/cdev.12936

11 Gürel, Ç., Brummelman, E., Sedikides, C., & Overbeek, G. (2020). Better than my past self: Temporal comparison raises children's pride without triggering superiority goals. *Journal of Experimental Psychology: General, 149*(8), 1554–66. https://doi.org/10.1037/xge0000733

12 Meltzoff, Andrew N., & Gilliam, Walter S. (2024). Young children & implicit racial biases. *Daedalus, 153*(1), 65–83. https://doi.org/https://doi.org/10.1162/daed_a_02

13 Wang, Y., & Benner, A. D. (2016 March). Cultural socialization across contexts: Family-peer congruence and adolescent well-being. *Journal of Youth and Adolescence, 45*(3), 594–611. https://doi.org/10.1007/s10964-016-0426-1. Epub 2016, January 25. PMID: 26809337; PMCID: PMC5353358.

14 The age of anxiety. (n.d.-b). *Washington Post*. https://www.washingtonpost.com/archive/lifestyle/wellness/2000/12/19/the-age-of-anxiety/300b209d-d217-4dbe-98cf-7a9d3b822420/

15 Gürel, Ç., Brummelman, E., Sedikides, C., & Overbeek, G. (2020). Better than my past self: Temporal comparison raises children's pride without triggering

superiority goals. *Journal of Experimental Psychology: General, 149*(8), 1554–66. https://doi.org/10.1037/xge0000733

16 Manning, R., Levine, M., & Collins, A. (2007). The Kitty Genovese murder and the social psychology of helping: The parable of the 38 witnesses. *American Psychologist, 62*(6), 555.

17 *Facts about bullying you need to know*. (n.d.). 3rdmil. https://3rdmil.com/facts_about_bullying_you_need_to_know/#:~:text=More%20than%20half%20(57%25),than%2020%25%20of%20the%20time.

18 *Physical punishment: Attitudes, behaviors, and norms*. (n.d.-a). Prevent Child Abuse America. https://preventchildabuse.org/wp-content/uploads/2021/05/Prevent-Child-Abuse-America-2021-Physical-Punishment-Report.pdf

19 Thensf. (2024, August 30). *How much sleep do you really need?* National Sleep Foundation. https://www.thensf.org/how-many-hours-of-sleep-do-you-really-need/

20 Mayo Foundation for Medical Education and Research. (2022, August 12). *Teen depression*. Mayo Clinic. https://www.mayoclinic.org/diseases-conditions/teen-depression/symptoms-causes/syc-20350985

Chapter 6

1 History and evolution of public education in the US. (n.d.-a). https://files.eric.ed.gov/fulltext/ED606970.pdf

2 Sussex Publishers. (n.d.). *Child development*. Psychology Today. https://www.psychologytoday.com/us/basics/child-development

3 Zauderer, S. (2023, August 24). *Lying statistics & facts: How often do people lie?* Life-Changing ABA Therapy—Cross River Therapy. https://www.crossrivertherapy.com/research/lying-statistics

4 McGill University. (2016, October 5). *The truth about lying? Children's perceptions get more nuanced with age*. Medical Xpress—medical research advances and health news. https://medicalxpress.com/news/2016-10-truth-lying-children-perceptions-nuanced.html

5 Arain, M., Haque, M., Johal, L., Mathur, P., Nel, W., Rais, A., Sandhu, R., & Sharma, S. (2013, April 3). Maturation of the adolescent brain. *Neuropsychiatric Disease and Treatment, 9*, 449–61. https://doi.org/10.2147/NDT.S39776. Epub. PMID: 23579318; PMCID: PMC3621648.

6. Arlin Cuncic, M. (2023, November 9). *What is triangulation in psychology?* Verywell Mind. https://www.verywellmind.com/what-is-triangulation-in-psychology-5120617

7. *An empirical examination of the effects of suspension and . . .* (n.d.-a). https://www.air.org/sites/default/files/2021-08/NYC-Suspension-Effects-Behavioral-Academic-Outcomes-August-2021.pdf

8. Staff, W. A. T. (2023, August 29). *What teachers need to know about restorative justice.* https://www.weareteachers.com/restorative-justice/

9. I and Wellbeing. (2024, January 8). *What is restorative practice?* Education. https://education.nsw.gov.au/schooling/school-community/attendance-behaviour-and-engagement/behaviour-support-toolkit/support-for-teachers/restorative-practices/restorative-practices

10. *Top 11 skills employers look for in job candidates.* (n.d.). indeed.com. https://www.indeed.com/career-advice/resumes-cover-letters/skills-employers-look-for

11. About Dr. Thomas Gordon. (n.d.). Gordon Training International. https://www.gordontraining.com/thomas-gordon/about-dr-thomas-gordon-1918-2002/

12. The Gottman Institute. (2024, March 5). *Gottman relationship recipes.* https://www.gottman.com/blog/gottman-relationship-recipes/

13. Irwin, M. (n.d.). *How to get your message across respectfully.* Describes how to use I-messages to communicate assertively. https://www.encouraging-appropriate-behaviour.com/free-stuff/how-to-use-i-messages.html

14. Costello, B., Wachtel, J., & Wachtel, T. (2019). *The restorative practices handbook: For teachers, Disciplinarians and administrators.* International Institute for Restorative Practices.

15. Joebrummer.com. (n.d.). https://www.joebrummer.com/2015/04/24/making-affective-statements-more-effective-in-restorative-practices/

16. Hannigan, J. D., & Hannigan, J. E. (2022). *Don't suspend me!: An alternative discipline toolkit.* Sage Publications Inc.

17. Kaczegowicz, C. (2023, March 10). *Creating a culture of empathy and accountability: The power of restorative justice in the classroom.* Medium. https://medium.com/practice-in-public/creating-a-culture-of-empathy-and-accountability-27fa2d3839eb

18. Gottman, J. S., & Gottman, J. M. (2024). *Fight right: How successful couples turn conflict into connection.* Harmony.

19. Costello, B., Wachtel, J., & Wachtel, T. (2019). *Restorative circles in schools: A practical guide for educators.* International Institute for Restorative Practices.

20 Google. (n.d.). *Why Singapore banned chewing gum*. Google. https://www.google.com/amp/s/www.bbc.com/news/magazine-32090420.amp

21 Parker-Pope, T. (2008, January 2). Teacher burnout? Blame the parents. *Well*. https://archive.nytimes.com/well.blogs.nytimes.com/2008/01/02/teacher-burnout-blame-the-parents/

22 Agrawal, S., & Marken, S. (2024, February 7). *K-12 workers have the highest burnout rate in U.S.* Gallup.com. https://news.gallup.com/poll/393500/workers-highest-burnout-rate.aspx

23 Centers for Disease Control and Prevention. (2023, April 27). *Youth Risk Behavior Surveillance System (YRBSS)*. https://www.cdc.gov/healthyyouth/data/yrbs/index.htm

24 *Kids offered coping skills at North Vegas School "Zen Den."* (n.d.). Retrieved December 12, 2022, from https://www.usnews.com/news/best-states/nevada/articles/2022-04-24/kids-offered-coping-skills-at-north-vegas-school-zen-den

25 Darlene Lancer, J. D. (2018, June 30). *Reality isn't always what you think! how cognitive distortions harm us*. Psych Central. Retrieved December 16, 2022, from https://psychcentral.com/lib/reality-isnt-always-what-you-think-how-cognitive-distortions-harm-us#1

26 *Children and egocentrism—education gateshead*. (n.d.). Retrieved December 13, 2022, from https://educationgateshead.org/wp-content/uploads/2021/09/3535b-JH-Children-And-Egocentrism.pdf

27 *More than 80 percent of U.S. public schools report that the pandemic has negatively impacted student behavior and socio-emotional development*. (n.d.). Press Release—More than 80 Percent of U.S. Public Schools Report Pandemic Has Negatively Impacted Student Behavior and Socio-Emotional Development—July 6, 2022. https://nces.ed.gov/whatsnew/press_releases/07_06_2022.asp

28 Novick, B. J. (2014, December). 15 ways to involve "at-risk parents." *NJEA Review*, 5(88), 28–9.

Chapter 7

1 Mischel, W., Zeiss, R., & Zeiss, A. (1974). Stanford preschool internal-external scale. *PsycTESTS Dataset*: n. pag. Web.

2 Novick, B. J. (2019). *The angry child: What parents, schools, and society can do*. Rowman & Littlefield.

3 Duckworth, A. L., Peterson, C., Matthews, M. D., & Kelly, D. R. (2007). Grit: Perseverance and passion for long-term goals. *Journal of Personality and Social Psychology*, *92*, 1087–101.

4   Nicola. (2020, December 7). *12 steps to teaching your child perseverance*. Minds of Wonder. Retrieved December 8, 2022, from https://mindsofwonder.com/2020/06/01/12-steps-to-teaching-your-child-perseverance/

5   *Character counts!* (2024, March 19). Character Counts! https://charactercounts.org/

6   Wallace, J. B. (2023). *Never enough when achievement culture becomes toxic—and what we can do about it*. Portfolio/Penguin.

7   Adams, P. D. (2022, November 21). *Relationships, resilience, and wellbeing: The science of gratitude: Umgc*. University of Maryland Global Campus. https://www.umgc.edu/blog/the-science-of-gratitude

8   What having a "growth mindset" actually means. (2023, April 6). *Harvard Business Review*. https://hbr.org/2016/01/what-having-a-growth-mindset-actually-means

9   Persona. (2024, April 8). *What is a growth mindset and how to develop it in 9 steps*. https://www.personatalent.com/development/how-to-cultivate-a-growth-mindset#:~:text=Developing%20a%20growth%20mindset%20requires,honed%20with%20effort%20and%20perseverance

Chapter 8

1   Arlin Cuncic, M. (2024, January 30). *What is a sense of entitlement?* Verywell Mind. https://www.verywellmind.com/what-is-a-sense-of-entitlement-5120616#:~:text=People%20with%20a%20sense%20of%20entitlement%20feel%20that%20they%20deserve,effort%20needed%20to%20do%20so

2   Clifton, J., & Hrynowski, Z. (2024, April 23). *How happy is gen Z?* Gallup.com. https://news.gallup.com/poll/643721/how-happy-gen-z.aspx

3   Moore, T. (2024, March 12). Mental health statistics 2024. *USA Today*. https://www.usatoday.com/money/blueprint/health-insurance/mental-health-statistics/#:~:text=But%20a%20large%20portion%20of,the%20most%20common%20mental%20illness?

4   American Psychological Association. (n.d.). *Anxiety*. American Psychological Association. https://www.apa.org/topics/anxiety

5   Hiroshima University. (2019, April 25). *Being too harsh on yourself could lead to OCD and anxiety*. ScienceDaily. Retrieved May 3, 2024 from www.sciencedaily.com/releases/2019/04/190425104253.htm

6   Hiroshima University. (2019, April 25). *Being too harsh on yourself could lead to OCD and anxiety*. ScienceDaily. Retrieved May 3, 2024 from www.sciencedaily.com/releases/2019/04/190425104253.htm

7   Gillis, A. S. (2023, June 6). *What is responsible AI?: Definition from TechTarget.* Enterprise AI. https://www.techtarget.com/searchenterpriseai/definition/responsible-AI#:~:text=Responsible%20AI%20is%20an%20approach,safe%2C%20trustworthy%20and%20ethical%20fashion

8   Education, U. C. for S. (n.d.). *Predictions of future global climate.* Center for Science Education. https://scied.ucar.edu/learning-zone/climate-change-impacts/predictions-future-global-climate

9   *Why climate change is so hard to tackle: The global problem.* (n.d.). https://www.axios.com/2019/08/19/why-climate-change-is-so-hard-to-tackle-the-global-problem

10 Baskin, K. (2019, December 27). *The 5 greatest challenges to fighting climate change.* MIT Sloan. https://mitsloan.mit.edu/ideas-made-to-matter/5-greatest-challenges-to-fighting-climate-change

11 Shabbir, R. (2024, May 8). *The future of education: 8 predictions for the next decade.* Educationise. https://educationise.com/post/the-future-of-education-8-predictions-for-the-next-decade/#:~:text=While%20teachers%20will%20always%20be,learn%20at%20their%20own%20pace.

12 Brotto, G. (2018, December 27). *The future of education depends on social emotional learning: Here's why—edsurge news.* EdSurge. https://www.edsurge.com/news/2018-06-04-the-future-of-education-depends-on-social-emotional-learning-here-s-why

13 *Leveraging technology to support social emotional learning (SEL).* (n.d.). CoSN. https://www.cosn.org/leveraging-technology-to-support-social-emotional-learning-sel/

14 Nearly two-thirds of young Americans fearful about the future of democracy in America, Harvard Youth Poll finds. (n.d.). The Institute of Politics at Harvard University. https://iop.harvard.edu/news/nearly-two-thirds-young-americans-fearful-about-future-democracy-america-harvard-youth-poll

15 Nadeem, R. (2023, September 19). *2. Views of the U.S. political system, the federal government and Federal-State relations.* Pew Research Center. https://www.pewresearch.org/politics/2023/09/19/views-of-the-u-s-political-system-the-federal-government-and-federal-state-relations/

Conclusion

1   Centers for Disease Control and Prevention. (2023, April 27). *Youth Risk Behavior Surveillance System (YRBSS).* https://www.cdc.gov/healthyyouth/data/yrbs/index.htm

2. Centers for Disease Control and Prevention. (2022, March 31). *New CDC data illuminate youth mental health threats during the COVID-19 pandemic.* https://www.cdc.gov/media/releases/2022/p0331-youth-mental-health-covid-19.html

3. Mhanj. (n.d.-a). https://www.mhanj.org/content/uploads/2021/08/NJHH-virtual-schedule-SEPTEMBER-2021-1.pdf

About the Author

Dr. Brett J. Novick holds a bachelor's degree in psychology, a master's degree in family therapy as well as post-degree work and certification in school social work, and a doctorate in educational leadership. Dr. Novick is licensed as a marriage and family therapist and state certified as a school social worker, supervisor, principal, and educational ddministrator and has been practicing and working in public schools and mental health for over twenty-five years.